Graphic Design for
Art
Fashion
Film
Architecture
Photography
Product Design
& Everything In Between

Graphic Design for
Art
Fashion
Film
Architecture
Photography
Product Design
& Everything In Between

Andy Cooke
Foreword by **Angharad Lewis**

PRESTEL
Munich · London · New York

CONT

ENTS

FOREWORD
Angharad Lewis

Most graphic designers are cultural gluttons, insatiably curious about the world. The best ones are those who can make sense of that curiosity, interpret it and communicate it. When their passions are put to work on a project, the result may speak quietly or loudly, use minimal means precisely handled, or put on a virtuoso performance of bold expressiveness. Either way, to succeed, each individual element must be in concert to communicate to an audience. That takes integrity on the part of the designer – the clarity of thought to understand what is needed from a project and the humility to prioritize the needs of the audience, whether that is to comfort or shock them.

There are nuances within this broad definition of 'good' graphic design, as this book seeks to showcase. The world needs designers who can excite and innovate, make work that illuminates subjects and ignites viewers. Graphic designers making such work are those who can conduct quality research, deftly interpret their findings, add their creative imagination to the mix and then execute their ideas with conviction and minute attention to detail.

In work for clients, graphic designers are routinely presented with challenges on a vast spectrum: a footwear company to rebrand, a theatre play to promote, a complex concept to distil, a simple fact to magnify. The way a designer makes sense of and approaches any given challenge is the backbone of her practice. Brilliant ideas do not come from thin air (or Pinterest). They are nurtured and fed by research, experience, analysis and experimentation. By its very nature, graphic design is a multifaceted discipline, meaning practitioners must be fluent across a range of skills, which often intersect with other types of creative work – photography, film, drawing, animation, editing and writing, to name but a few.

Graphic designers are, to an extent, the polymaths of the creative world. Each project can bring them into contact with a new subject, new materials, a new industry, new people, new messages. Each project sees the designer calling on acquired knowledge but also hunting for new knowledge: what are the values most prized by this industry? How can I adapt this platform for a new audience? How does this paper perform with this ink? What are the limits I can push this material to?

This book tells the story of the processes and approaches behind projects for creative clients by some top-class graphic designers. It is often in work for clients from the worlds of art, fashion, film, photography, architecture and product design that we see graphic designers come most alive. The richness and quality of the content they have to grapple with and the possibilities opened up by collaboration with visually fluent clients make such projects the coveted work of any design studio and, often, the ones they are most proud to share with the world. But projects for creative clients also come with a unique set of difficulties and anxieties, as the interviews in this book touch upon. However, there is no doubt that visual communication in this context presents a vanguard worth following.

Angharad Lewis is co-editor of Grafik.net, a leading resource for the world's most inspiring graphic design. She writes about design and culture for various publications and is also a lecturer at the Cass School of Art, Architecture and Design. She lives and works in London.

INTRODUCTION
Andy Cooke

'If you can design one thing, you can design everything.'
– Massimo Vignelli

The creative industries fascinate me, with graphic design sparking particular interest. After all, it's my day-to-day – I wouldn't be much of a graphic designer if I wasn't intrigued by it. Working within this sector, however, for and with clients that span a multitude of disciplines, can sometimes create a bubble of self-righteousness; narcissism mixed with delusions of grandeur. In the outside world, creative careers tend to get pushed down the list of viable options for young people, regarded as a lesser form compared to traditional academic subjects and seen as a risky move if one wants to be financially successful. My own stepfather recently admitted he was initially unconvinced of my attraction to design both as a youngster and at degree level, and thought I should have ventured down a route that involved a time-honoured trade instead, such as building or plumbing.

Maybe that's just a generational thing; but the political view of creative fields tends to be lacklustre in countries like the UK and US too, with school and public arts programmes frequently threatened with being axed in favour of more 'conventional' subjects. Generally, this is met with dismay and anger (and rightly so), leading to petitions and outcries about the societal and economic importance of the arts and creative endeavours as well as their relevance to personal expression and well-being.

It might just be the bubble I've formed within my social circles, both online and in reality, but the graphic design community seems to be among those at the forefront of this ongoing conversation, with war cries loud and proud about how imperative our practice is to people's daily lives. That said, many of us inwardly question our own importance: 'Why would anyone want to read about graphic design?' Adrian Shaughnessy writes in the introduction to his book of essays *Scratching the Surface*. There's no doubt that the considered use of graphic design for businesses, initiatives and projects of all kinds is imperative, and embracing a strategic approach to brand identities, websites, mobile applications, collateral materials and experiences falls under that umbrella. While designers working in the creative industries need to be just that – creative – they must also be commercially savvy so that the fields in question can continue to thrive and provide realistic career options for people at any stage of their professional lives.

      With this book, I was keen to look further into graphic design's overall significance and how it operates within the cultural sector. Most weeks, I see a project launched by a designer or studio I admire and I immediately like the work, too. Half the time it's been done for another creative entity, which stimulates further appeal (along with pushing me to do better work myself). But it often makes me think: has this incredible piece of design been through the same process as, say, a branding job for a financial institution?

      I have chosen a wide range of disciplines here to obtain a broad viewpoint on design executions across them, including art, fashion, film, architecture, photography, product design and more. I've included my own thoughts on how and why the projects featured here succeed within these categories, too. I've also interviewed some of today's leading creatives, asking them a series of questions not just about the work in the book, but about what happens when graphic designers collaborate with other artists, designers and makers. There are opposing theories regarding the same questions, as well as insights that align across the board, resulting in plenty of food for thought for graphic designers to question their approach and process when dealing with creative versus non-creative clients. For example, there is sometimes a need to educate a client to understand the reasons for a particular choice – why a certain colour palette is best for an identity, or why a certain typeface was selected – but does that same type of discussion occur when the client is already design-savvy? Some say yes, some say no, and that's the wonderful thing: everybody has an opinion on these matters. I invite you to form your own.

The term 'commercial art' has often been used to define what graphic design is within particular circles, especially before 'graphic design' itself was coined. Although this may be an overly simplified way of explaining a complex process that entails juggling consumer mind-sets, semiotics and behaviours along with strategy, design systems and multiple marketing touchpoints, it does serve a purpose in that it can help clarify the difference between graphic design and fine art, which is usually created for its own sake.

Graphic designers working within the art world like to explore and produce abstract concepts. The sector encourages free-form thinking and is thus sometimes envied by designers operating within contrasting, non-creative industries. Yet, over time, these vastly different fields have warmed up to the fact that experimental ideas can, and do, succeed for many types of identity systems. What results is much more than trends, but trust: nowadays, a growing number of clients are giving designers room to push boundaries in historically traditional arenas. As part of the creative process, designers frequently include striking, memorable works of art in their research and reference materials for projects.

ArtRabbit

by Bond

Founded in 2009 and with studios in Helsinki, Abu Dhabi and London, Bond is a creative agency focused on design and branding across digital, identity, spatial, retail, packaging and products. Using a designer-driven approach, the agency brings together talented practitioners from a variety of fields, generating projects that span multiple disciplines for brands like Microsoft, University of the Arts Helsinki, Moomin and Dubai Design Week.

ArtRabbit, a website and mobile app that neatly catalogues contemporary art exhibitions around the world, approached Bond in 2014 when in need of an updated identity. Using the concept of 'turning art on its head' as the main driver of the design, the execution, involving an upside-down 'R' that looks like a rabbit's head, is witty and memorable. As a logo, it almost seems to speak to what 'art' is – evident especially when it is overprinted onto pre-existing T-shirts. It operates almost like a seal of approval in that, when stamped, viewers may realize something is art that they didn't previously consider as such, opening up pathways of discovery and appreciation.

Interview with Hugh Miller and Ty Lou,
co-founders and creatives at Bond

Do you think that crossing multiple design disciplines is a viable approach to working within the industry today?

People's interests and skills differ. Some have a wide range of interests and an ability to stretch over many fields; others are more niche and prefer to specialize in one area. There is no right or wrong. We enjoy crossing disciplines, pushing the limits. We are a diverse group of designers, each bringing a specific set of skills and specialisms to the table. We value working with people outside our fields. Nurturing a collaborative approach and building lasting relationships with clients and colleagues broadens your experience and creates new opportunities as you explore new ground.

Does your design process differ when you're dealing with a client
within the creative industries?

> When working with other creatives the progress happens at a much
> faster pace, as you don't need to educate them. On a practical
> level, there is less need to prepare presentations or convince them
> about your approach, as other creatives tend to be in sync. But each
> project comes with its own unique set of rules and challenges.

Every potential client now has access to software that can output
graphic design, in some form, at their fingertips. How has this
impacted the way we design for design-savvy clients?

> A client with design knowledge and access to design tools can
> technically be considered a designer. The design quality that they
> are able to produce depends on how much they have mastered
> the craft. Effectively, using the tools is only part of the job;
> critical elements are experience, knowledge of the medium and
> understanding human behaviour.
>   Any client that comes to us, including creative clients,
> is looking for a certain quality of work and an outside perspective.
> Each project is different and budget constraints mean that
> sometimes the client takes over design work directly. In cases like
> that we make sure we set tight guidelines to help us manage
> quality control.

Do clients in the creative industries often want to respond to
current trends in their respective fields?

> We tend to think of trends as patterns that emerge out of a
> constantly changing world. There are so many influences that
> create trends: the economy, science, technology, politics and so
> on. Trends are definitely an influence when clients commission
> projects. While working with ArtRabbit, our conversation was
> heavily influenced by discussions around open source and open,
> democratic processes as being critical for contemporary culture.

'We tend to think of trends as
patterns that emerge out of a
constantly changing world.'

Do you think clients are more likely to hire a studio or designer that
has won awards?

> Awards can be compelling to new clients; they can give some extra
> reassurance and confidence in the agency's abilities. Our awards
> cabinet is strategically placed in full view for when clients walk
> through the door! But jokes aside, we never approach a project
> with a certain award or competition in mind; that would be such
> a distraction. When you're working with a client, especially a new
> client, you're focused on solving a design problem and finding
> strong solutions – often with a limited timeframe or under other
> constraints. It's only when the project is over and you come up for
> air that you think: 'Maybe this will resonate with the Type Directors
> Club,' for example (as did the ArtRabbit identity).

How much does the design industry influence design
decisions as part of the creative process when working with
creatively led clients?

> This really depends on the project. For some projects you don't
> need to reinvent the wheel but instead focus on specific areas that
> can be improved, such as functionality, visual language and design
> strategy. Generally, with creative clients, there is already a sense
> of understanding, a common ground, and you set the bar higher
> inherently as you embark on a collaborative journey. In the case of
> ArtRabbit, we were one team thrashing out ideas quickly. We would
> build on each other's thoughts.

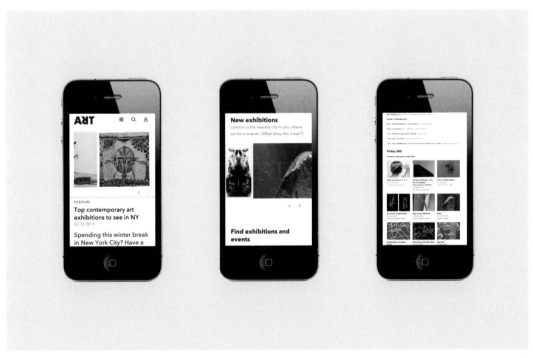

ARTRABBIT
.COM

'We wanted to help people browse art and pick shows they'd like to see, preparing their own "trails" and hopping from one place to the next, armed with the curiosity, playfulness and confidence of a rabbit.'

Interview with ArtRabbit's founder and director
Tom Elsner and managing editor Vivi Kallinikou

When and why did you decide to commission Bond to help
with your rebrand?

When we set out to create a practical guide to contemporary art
events, the idea of an 'art rabbit' came up in a conversation about
myriad voices and fast-spreading phenomena. We all immediately
loved the name; it seemed both iconic and accessible. We wanted
to help people browse art and pick shows they'd like to see,
preparing their own 'trails' and hopping from one place to the next,
armed with the curiosity, playfulness and confidence of a rabbit.

ArtRabbit is all about combining serendipity and
intention in exploring art. In 2014, we started transforming our
service with a rebranding process. While the previous brand was
overpowering, dominating the content, we were now looking for
a brand experience that communicated ArtRabbit as an open
network; a brand that acted as a recognizable mark but felt
inclusive and left enough breathing space for the crowdsourced
content. Bond did such a fantastic job translating this sentiment
to the ArtRabbit brand.

Do you think your own understanding of graphic design can affect
the design process, as a client?

Every client, creative or not, comes with a unique set of skills
that impacts the development of the design process. We have a
background in graphic and web design and art theory, and work
within a complex, self-critical cultural context. We know how
graphic design impacts a brand's spirit and recognize its power to
communicate a message effectively. With this in mind, we were able
to provide a more detailed brief [to Bond] – including a critique of
the existing brand from both a strategic and visual perspective –
and a brand story outlining our mission. This accelerated the design
process and led to a very fruitful collaboration.

As design-savvy clients yourselves, what was it like working with
outside creatives on your rebrand?

When we commissioned Bond to rebrand ArtRabbit, we were
looking for a collaboration and a fresh pair of eyes. Working on our
launch exhibition concept illustrates this well. While discussing
our work with Bond and going through our user-generated content
on the ArtRabbit website, we came up with what later became the
centrepiece of our exhibition. A poster wall displayed hundreds of
exhibition titles from our database. Contemporary art exhibitions
have the quirkiest, at times even nonsensical titles. You can
attend events like 'You Dig the Tunnel, I'll Hide the Soil', 'Through
Your Door Everything Turns and Sits in Circles' or 'YouTube Killed
the Video Star' – this game of words is a gift to a designer! The
exhibition concept was as simple as it was appealing: each poster
represented one voice from the ArtRabbit platform and the poster
wall represented the multitude of voices. Our brand values and our
service were immediately translated into an exhibition concept.

What would your advice be for a graphic designer or studio aiming
to specialize in the creative industries, from a client's point of view?

Working for the creative industries is an attractive proposition
because you get exposed to beautiful, valuable aesthetic objects
and ideas. Good design must serve – not overpower – them. The
best approach in order to thrive within the creative community
is to answer every brief strategically and then intuitively. Absorb
information from the client, understand their message and their
story, what they've set out to do, why they look the way they do.
Then, translate their message into good design.

How do you see graphic design's role in the wider creative industries, traditionally and in the future?

The term 'visual communication' describes the traditional role of a graphic designer very well. Today, and more so in the future, graphic designers work in a wider context. There are many touchpoints for a brand that are not visual, or only partly visual. A brand is expressed as the interactive experience on a website, the tone of voice on other channels, like social media or a customer help system, and it evolves over time; it's not static. Therefore, a more conceptual, strategic and multidisciplinary approach to graphic design is key: understand the medium, take human behaviour into account, apply design thinking to the wider context to provide the best possible brand experience.

'Working for the creative industries is an attractive proposition because you get exposed to beautiful, valuable aesthetic objects and ideas. Good design must serve – not overpower – them.'

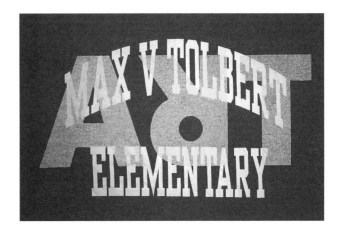

Edouard Malingue Gallery

by Lundgren+Lindqvist

Graphic design studio Lundgren+Lindqvist, founded in 2007 and based in Gothenburg, Sweden, have built a solid reputation within the international design community for their work within art direction, print, digital, identity design, packaging design, web development and signage. Whether it's for small creative clients (like laptop and tablet case brand MCKNGBRD) or international corporations (such as Coca-Cola), independently or in tandem with outside designers and agencies, Lundgren+Lindqvist take a conceptual approach to their projects and have become recognized for devising compelling ideas and putting them into practice in a visually arresting way.

Edouard Malingue Gallery, established in 2010 in Hong Kong to exhibit contemporary art, approached Lundgren+Lindqvist for a full overhaul of their identity to coincide with a move to a larger space in 2015. The system the designers came up with revolves around the number three, seen in its most basic form as three solid, bold strokes in the logo. The 'trisection', as it has been labelled, is an abstract reference to the three words in the gallery's name, as well as to the three lines needed to make a legible 'E' (for Edouard) and 'M' (for Malingue). The trisection is used liberally within various aspects of the identity, most cleverly to dictate the overall grid applied to a range of applications, as well as for the number of folds of collateral materials like posters, leaflets and letters. To continue this theme, the gallery's website is built around three columns.

Edouard Malingue Gallery est heureuse de présenter l'exposition Future Archeology, premier spectacle de Laurent Grasso en Asie depuis Esprit Radio agnès b de. Galerie du jour à Hong Kong, Chine en 2003, dans les premiers jours de sa carrière internationale.

Au-delà de son aura romantique, l'exposition Future Archeology joue avec la notion de temps qui apparaît ici comme comprimé, créant pour Laurent Grasso une déstabilisation même paranoïaque, effet. Cette tension ne cesse de repousser plus loin vers certaines limites de la perception du spectateur, comme quand il prétend que sa série de tableaux études du passé sont prises à partir de la Renaissance italienne ou les âges classiques de la peinture européenne. De même son néon contemporaine œuvre d'art Stella Nova se réfère à un siècle 17e essai sur une étoile filante. Cette exposition sera l'occasion de démontrer comment le travail de cet artiste a mûri avec une sélection d'oeuvres d'art soigneusement organisée couvrant plus de toute une carrière.

En plus de l'exposition au sein de la galerie, Laurent Grasso va installer son pavillon anéchoïque, une cabane d'une pièce construite comme un lieu de méditation et l'observation des environs, sur le toit de Ferry Central Pier 4, en face du port de Victoria. Cette pièce emblématique permettra aux visiteurs de découvrir une sensation unique de l'exploration intérieure. Les visiteurs pourront embarquer pour un voyage de les prendre du coeur de la ville la plus active dans le monde pour en marge de la réalité et la fiction.

Né en France en 1972, Laurent Grasso est universellement considéré comme l'un des artistes les plus importants de sa génération. Avant entrepris sa carrière couronnée de succès dans les années 2000, d'ici 2008, il avait reçu le prestigieux prix Marcel Duchamp. Ceci constitue la plus importante exposition solo de l'artiste à ce jour et sera ensuite voyager au Musée d'Art Contemporain de Montréal, Canada.

Edouard Malingue Gallery is pleased to present Future Archeology, Laurent Grasso's first show in Asia since Radio Studio's gallery du jour in Hong Kong, China in 2003 in the early days of his international career.

Beyond its romantic aura, Future Archeology plays with the notion of time what appears here as compressed, creating for Laurent Grasso a destabilising, even paranoid, effect. This tension continually pushes further towards certain boundaries of the spectator's perception such as when he pretends that his series of paintings Studies from the Past are taken from the Italian Renaissance or the classical ages of European painting. Similarly his contemporary neon Stella Nova refers to a 17th century essay about a shooting star. This exhibition will be the occasion to demonstrate how the work of this artist has matured with a carefully curated selection of artworks.

In addition to the exhibition within the gallery, Laurent Grasso will install his Anechoic Pavilion, a one-room cabin constructed as a place for meditation and observation of surroundings, on the rooftop of Central Ferry Pier 4, facing the Victoria Harbour. This iconic piece will allow visitors to experience a unique sensation of inner exploration. Visitors will embark on a journey taking them from the heart of the most active city in the world to the very margins of reality and fiction.

Born in France in 1972, Laurent Grasso is universally regarded as one of the most prominent artists of his generation. Having embarked upon his successful career in the early 2000s, by 2008 he had been awarded the prestigious Marcel Duchamp Prize. This constitutes the artist's most important solo exhibition to date and will subsequently travel to the Musée d'Art Contemporain de Montréal, Canada.

Future Archeology

Laurent Grasso

26.04–16.06.15

≡ edouardmalingue.com

6th Floor, 33 Des Voeux Road Central, HK

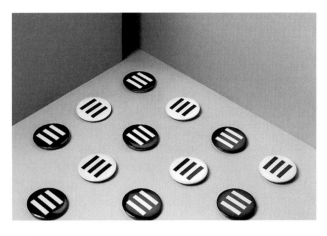
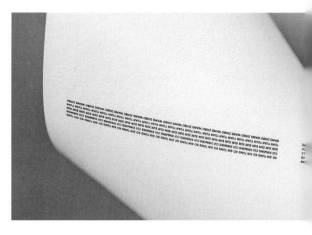
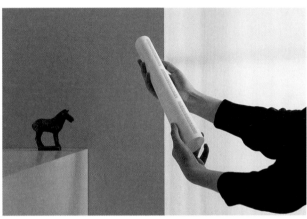

Do you think that crossing multiple design disciplines is a viable approach to working within the industry today?

Interview with Andreas Friberg Lundgren, art director and co-founder of Lundgren+Lindqvist

One of the things that attracted me to pursuing a career as a graphic designer was the idea that it would allow me to take a cross-disciplinary approach to what I do. Some days, I will work on developing a visual identity system, while others I may art direct a photoshoot or discuss the functionality of a digital product we are working on with one of our developers. As a studio and through our clients, we are constantly exposed to new challenges. We work with a varied range of businesses, local and international, from art galleries and publishers to clients in fashion and tech start-ups. These clients of course have very varied needs, and while we might design an e-commerce platform for one, another may need a system for extending their visual identity to their office space. The approach is not very different from that of architects like Arne Jacobsen, who would start from the macro, by designing the building, and finish in micro by designing the cutlery for the building's restaurant.

However much I wish that we had time to do it all, we also have to face the fact that we are a fairly small studio and as such there are limits to what we can do. We also really enjoy collaborating with our extended network of architects, artists, photographers and writers.

Does your design process differ when you're dealing with a client within the creative industries?

Sometimes it does, largely depending on how the client's business and process relates to our own. With clients within the creative industries, the dialogue is often more informed when it comes to questions relating to creative matters. This allows us to shortcut the process of explaining certain things that would be expected and required by a client in another business segment, giving us more time to focus on the actual work. In many cases our process is also informed by the client's approach, and in some cases we may also make use of their services to strengthen the project.

How important is graphic design to the wider design industry?

Graphic design has long resided in the shadow of disciplines like architecture or furniture design, largely due to the fact that these disciplines are easier to relate and react to for people outside the industry.

Over the last few years, this situation has started to change, exemplified by the massive public reactions (not to say uproar) following the rebranding campaigns of popular brands such as GAP and Airbnb. This has also affected the seriousness with which graphic design is discussed in the wider design industry.

ne of the things that attracted me
pursuing a career as a graphic
esigner was the idea that it would
low me to take a cross-disciplinary
pproach to what I do.'

Do you see defined professions within the design industry being
blurred by particular practitioners?

> One example, which we see to an increasing extent, is graphic
> designers teaming up with web developers and entrepreneurs to
> create new, online-based products and applications. I think this
> type of set-up makes perfect sense, as projects of that nature tend
> to require an open-ended design process to keep up with technical
> developments and consumers' requests.

Do you find working with clients in the creative industries to
be easier or harder than working with non-creatives?

> Cross-disciplinary buyer/client relationships can sometimes
> mean opposing views and strong opinions on both sides. At times,
> a client within a neighbouring discipline will have an idea of how
> they should be portrayed. Sometimes this standpoint is one that
> we share, but in other cases we may have a contrasting view. This is
> where a sense of mutual trust becomes really important. We must
> trust our client to be experts on their business, while they must
> trust us to be experts on ours. Over the years, we have found that
> our most successful projects are the ones where there is a strong
> sense of shared trust. As a consequence of this, we work very hard
> to establish a relationship built upon that foundation from the
> outset of every new project.
> To us, every studio–client relationship means a constant
> transmission of information back and forth. As much as we will
> sometimes have to inform our client in questions related to our
> practice, in the end, they will have likely have 'educated' us to a
> greater extent than vice versa.

Do you feel designers must expand their technology-based
skill sets to stay relevant?

We have certainly seen an increase in motion graphics as a natural
component of visual identity systems designed over the last few
years. In many cases, it has seemed like the urge to animate a
logotype has been stronger than the idea behind the animation. In
other cases, the application has felt like a natural progression and
as such the introduction of motion has made the visual identity
stronger. For many illustrators, motion has also been a logical
extension of their craft, as onscreen displays of their work replace
it being published in print to an increasing extent.

Although the progress has been slower than is perhaps
desirable (and certainly in relation to our expectations), we are also
seeing many young graphic designers with skills as web developers,
and vice versa. Since the processes of designing and developing for
online applications are so intertwined, it makes perfect sense to
us to be able to do both.

'or many illustrators, motion has
lso been a logical extension of their
raft, as onscreen displays of their
vork replace it being published in
rint to an increasing extent.'

Is a traditional knowledge of and approach to graphic design
still applicable in today's creative landscape?

Yes and no. The basic principles stay roughly the same but the
circumstances change, and as a result graphic design must remain
in a state of constant adaptation. Today it seems that many design
students lack sufficient education in the basics of graphic design,
such as building and using grids or kerning typography. This is likely
a result of many educational institutions' struggles to keep up with
the swift and sudden changes in the expectations of the students
on behalf of future employers. We hope that the coming years will
bring a balance that allows time both for learning the basics and
keeping up with new, exciting developments.

Haus der Kunst

by Base

Base, founded in 1997, is an ideas-led agency with offices in New York, Brussels and Geneva. Through this international lens the team apply a clear ten-point manifesto and approach to each of their projects, adhering to tenets like: 'We don't design for designers. We design for people', 'We freely mix our creative disciplines' and 'We are not afraid to make mistakes. We learn from them.' Base's impressive roster of clients also spans the globe, ranging from the cultural, music and sports industries to the Museum of Sex in New York, Fondation Louis Vuitton, JFK Airport's Terminal 4 and the city of Brussels.

The building in which Munich's Haus der Kunst museum resides was erected in 1937 as an example of Nazi architecture. In fitting defiance of this fact, it is now a home to contemporary art. This paradox has translated into the visual identity that Base developed for the museum in 2012, based on the concept of multiple viewpoints. The phrase 'Stretch Your View' was devised as a touchstone that props up the design system, at the centre of which is an inquisitive, curious logo that takes many forms across a multitude of formats and outputs. This stretchable system aims to encourage viewers to look at things from various angles and perspectives, echoing the strategies of progressive art. The idea of constant movement and energy is also implied, as the identity expands and contracts.

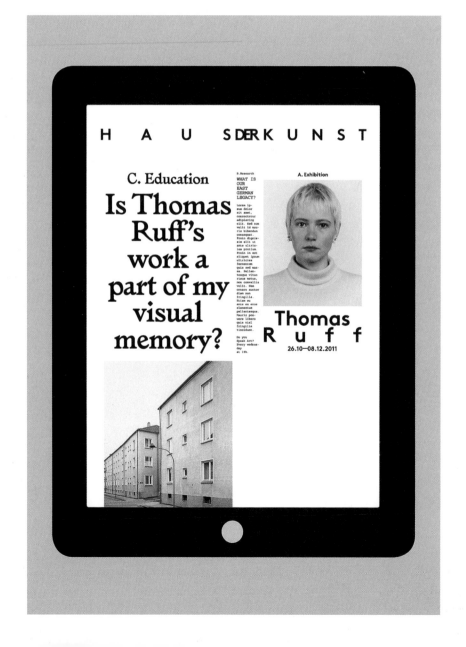

This project came about around the time that responsive, flexible identities were beginning to emerge from some of the world's biggest companies – an indication of the way branding is headed in the future. Sometimes, these mutable design systems can feel forced and 'for the sake of it'; Base's work for Haus der Kunst, however, is clearly grounded in solid design thinking and evidently not a product of ill-considered attempts to follow current trends.

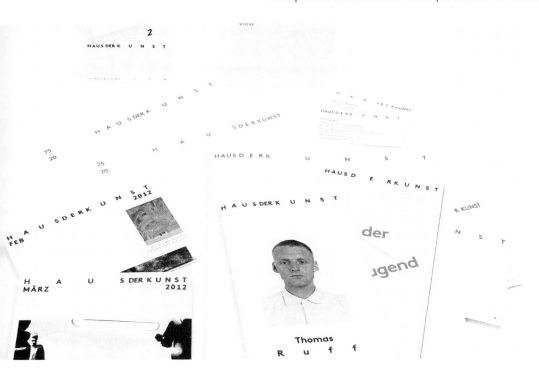

ArtDate

by Studio Temp

Studio Temp was founded in 2007 in the small city of Bergamo, Italy, by a trio of childhood friends. They work across art direction, identity, website design and exhibition design for local and international brands and institutions. And through their strong links to Mousse Publishing, the designers have collaborated with some of the greatest contemporary art institutions, artists, curators and museums on exhibition catalogues, monographs and artists' books.

In 2016, Bergamo-based The Blank, a cultural association focused on spreading curiosity about contemporary art, commissioned Studio Temp to conceive an identity for their annual ArtDate festival. Each year, this event brings a weekend of immersive art-related happenings to the city, from studio visits to performances, lectures and exhibitions in unconventional spaces. The idea of blank space was used as a jumping-off point for the main identity, focusing on the concept of empty blocks (and recalling The Blank's name).

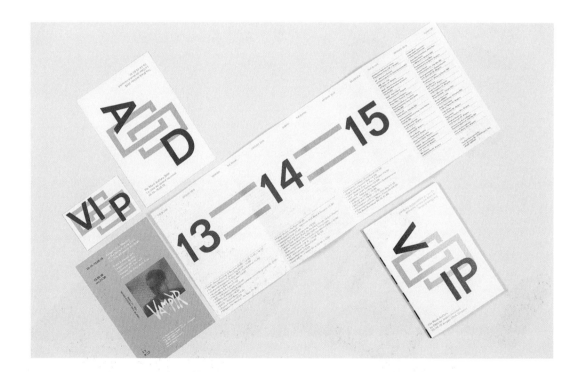

White space is something that is often found within graphic design solutions for art, just as galleries frequently use blank white walls as backdrops to showcase work effectively and clearly. Thus the muted colour palette of the ArtDate identity is no accident, and the introduction of bronze as a special colour gives it an air of prestige. Combined with heavy, reductive typography surrounded by white space on the pages, it communicates in a direct way.

COMUNE DI BERGAMO
Servizio
Pubbliche
Affissioni
The Blank ArtDate
La Città dei destini incrociati
13–14–15 maggio 2016
Le giornate dell'Arte Contemporanea
30 eventi a Bergamo
programma: www.theblank.it
Le giornate dell'Arte Contemporanea
30 eventi a Bergamo
programma: www.theblank.it
13–14–15 maggio 2016

THE BLANK
ARTDATE
THREE   OF
DAYS
CONTEMPORARY   ART

The 6th Edition is inspired by Italo Calvino's book "Il castello dei destini incrociati" and the Visconti-Sforza tarot deck.

HIGHLIGHTS 6TH EDITION:
• Special Talks - Emanuela Daffra, Paolo Fabbri, Umberto Galimberti, William Voelkle
• GAMeC - Dear Betty: Run Fast, Bite Hard! curated by Lucrezia Calabrò Visconti
• BACO Project Space - James Hoff: Black Box curated by Stefano Raimondi and Mauro Zanchi
• BACO Base Arte Contemporanea - Oscar Giaconia: Green Room curated by Stefano Raimondi and Mauro Zanchi
• Live Soundtrack Performance: Amp Rive perform a live soundtrack for Vampyr (C. Th. Dreyer, 1932)
• MASBEDO - unrealased performance

The Blank ArtDate 2016
La Città dei destini incrociati
13–14–15 May 2016, Bergamo

annuale dedicato all'Arte
Blank propone al pubblico di
rato dagli spazi espositivi visitati
manifestazione (13-14-15 maggio 2016).

e della sesta edizione di ArtDate, il
destini incrociati" di Italo Calvino, a
vo presente in programma è stata associata
di tarocchi Visconti-Sforza, in parte conservato
ara di Bergamo.

rare dalle carte, dalle opere d'Arte Contemporanea
lla storia del mazzo, crea un racconto e invialo a The
l 15 giugno 2016.

nazioni su ArtDate e sulle categorie in concorso,
amento e le scadenze, consulta il bando sul sito
theblank.it

The Blank Contemporary Art
www.theblank.it

TR

eblank.it

NS

The Blank TR – Transit Message

AF

The Blank TR –

Art Museum at the University of Toronto
by Underline Studio

The designers at Underline Studio, founded in 2005 and based in Toronto, Canada, work with an intentionally diverse range of clients, including Random House, Google and Harvard Medical School, finding a sweet spot between the cultural, corporate, education, retail and publishing sectors. They blend classic and cutting-edge thinking across art direction and design of visual identities, marketing materials, books, packaging, and interactive and motion graphics.

In 2014 the University of Toronto Art Centre and Justina M. Barnicke Gallery were combined to form the Art Museum at the University of Toronto, becoming one of the metropolis's largest gallery spaces. Now operating as a single entity, the museum sought Underline's help in creating a new brand identity that would emphasize the institution's placement within the city as well as its aim to draw in the university community and the greater Toronto public alike. In response, Underline built an identity system around the concept of an angled logo, set at the same 16.7-degree angle as Toronto's street grid, making it a literal product of its environment. It functions across a range of promotional materials, from banners and brochures to programmes, posters and the museum's website.

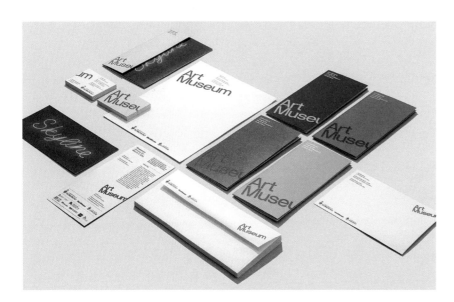

Art Museum at the University of Toronto by Underline Studio

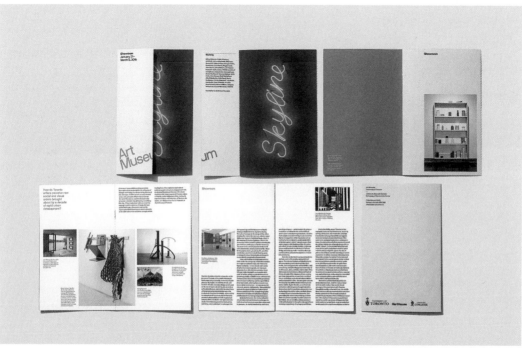

This modest idea can be applied nicely to different media and formats, with the angled logo often being cropped, cut or split up across multiple printed assets. It also helps to enforce the coming together of the pre-existing art centre and gallery – a subtle reference, but one that gives sound justification for pushing the logo to an abstract place that could make some clients uncomfortable. The memorable, daring and very much unique colour palette takes this one step further. But, this is art – and by offsetting the colours with clear and clinical typography, it balances out appropriately.

FASI

At design schools worldwide, the idea of producing trend-led work is often met with disdain and reluctance. Instead, the concept of the 'timeless' piece of graphic design that transcends generations is perpetuated: for a brand, this means endless consistency, no matter the decade or relevance, as audiences grow with their products.

On the flip side, fashion doesn't align with this thinking. It moves as time moves, occasionally harking back twenty or so years to inspire new waves of trends that take multiple sources as their inspiration. Collaborating with the fashion world is a challenge that some graphic designers avoid, as it flies in the face of how they were trained. Others, however, are able to embrace shifting tides and capture the zeitgeist. Certain design studios are renowned for their trend-led approach; others are recognized for defining what's in style where others follow, consciously or otherwise.

Working alongside some of the greatest minds in fashion opens up opportunities for graphic designers to push boundaries like they do when working with clients in the art world, but in a different way, as fashion-based clients are constantly seeking new ways to stand apart in the consumer marketplace. Indeed, it can be a place where designers can scratch a particular creative itch and enjoy making beautiful work that also satisfies the urge to stay in vogue.

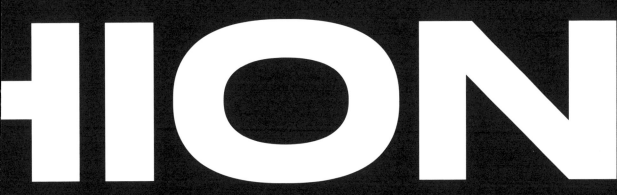

Augustus Pili

by Koto

Koto, a relatively young outfit based in south London, have already worked with a roster of huge, internationally known clients, including Airbnb, Fanta and Gumtree. In the short period since the studio's founding in 2014, the Koto team have achieved great success by taking care to obtain a thorough understanding of a brand's essence, bringing a clear, distinct approach to every design solution.

In 2015, self-taught footwear designer Jalil Rahman launched his shoe brand Augustus Pili, asking Koto to create an identity for the business. Rahman's aim was to start a brand that would reflect his own personality and experiences. His signature style involves a combination of striking colour choices, contemporary design and juxtaposing fabrics, with handmade British craftsmanship as the main driving principle.

This vision is well and truly communicated through Koto's exciting and vibrant brand identity, which puts the product first without overshadowing the craft that has gone into making the shoes. The contrast between the almost engraved semi-serif of the word 'Augustus' and the organic, hand-rendered 'Pili' for the core logo rounds off a successful design system. It can be challenging for designers to work with clients who are so heavily invested in their own companies. Yet, with such an idiosyncratic client, it's evident that Koto were able to get at the brand's ethos, encapsulating Rahman's personal and corporate values.

Interview with Jowey Roden,
co-founder of Koto

Does your design process differ when you're dealing with a client within the creative industries?

We don't really work to a prescribed process, regardless of the job or client. Agencies can be guilty of forcing their own process on clients instead of understanding their needs and building a process accordingly.
　　　　We work with clients that possess creative expertise, and others that excel in leadership, marketing or innovation. Each is unique in the way they dictate our relationship and how we ultimately work together. Occasionally we have to guide our collaborators through the creative process, and in other relationships it is implicitly understood.

How important is graphic design to the wider design industry?

Design can change the way we live, the way our businesses are run and the majority of our daily interactions. There are multiple tools that can incite and be a vessel for this change: product design, industrial design, graphic design and a whole lot more. Each is a tool to resolve a problem or to present an idea. None of these is more important [than the others], just at times more relevant.

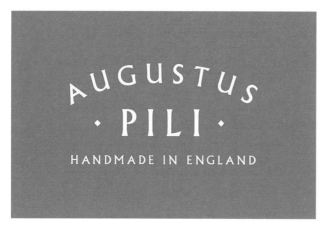

'Our hope is that we imbue everything we make with ideas that ultimately live beyond trends, because brilliant ideas are always relevant regardless of timescale.'

How do trends affect the working process with creative clients who want to stay relevant and in tune with the zeitgeist?

To deny visual trends is to kid yourself, as they are so obviously present in everyday visual culture. As technology gets faster, better and cheaper, our aesthetic follows. You need only look at a decade-old monitor or TV to see how quickly these changes in aesthetics happen. For clients chasing the zeitgeist it can be appropriately managed by considering two things: ideas and appropriateness. Our hope is that we imbue everything we make with ideas that ultimately live beyond trends, because brilliant ideas are always relevant regardless of timescale.

Appropriateness comes into play when you consider the product and its market. Snapchat warrants an incredibly contemporary aesthetic because it's targeted at millennials. They can understand a complex product, and if they don't they are willing to discover it. A contemporary art gallery exhibiting modern work is deserving of a 'trendy' identity because it aligns with its product. Similarly, the identity for a gallery that exhibits Picasso and Rembrandt need only be aware of its heritage to tailor its identity accordingly.

Design projects often get press attention in design circles, which helps to showcase creators in the industry. Can this also attract clients from outside industries?

The design press is in decline. I can only theorize, but I believe the reason for this is threefold. First, designers aren't very good at being nice to one another. Second, the fetishization of typography and design beauty has grown tired. Lastly, social media has changed the way we consume. If the intent for any work is to impress the design community, it's already failed in properly representing the business, product, service or content it carries.

Clients and collaborators can absolutely appreciate beauty – some of our clients are designers themselves – however, I don't believe it's the most important box to tick. More so, can I have a relationship with this person? Will their work support the growth of our business? Will they make responsible choices for our brand? Aesthetics are short-lived. Make it beautiful, but above all else make it work.

How much can one realistically apply learning and skills across
different design disciplines in the commercial world?

> The majority of us practise a craft. That craft can be broad:
> businessperson, entrepreneur, executive, director; or more targeted:
> designer, engineer, mathematician, salesperson. Our craft generally
> shapes the way we see the world. No craft is better than another.
> At times one might be more appropriate, but each is just a different
> way of seeing.
>   Design is absolutely applicable across multiple
> commercial disciplines. Whatever your craft is, utilizing it as
> your basic approach to problem-solving and business can be an
> incredibly productive and authentic methodology for success,
> regardless of sector. It doesn't necessarily matter what your craft
> is, what's important is that you have one and are bloody good at it.

How do you see graphic design's role in the wider creative
industries, traditionally and in the future?

> Graphic design is a tool, like any other discipline. It can mean
> typesetting a menu, designing an advert or building an entire
> brand. Traditionally, graphic design has been concerned with beauty,
> reduction and rule. It's the wrapping and the polish.
>   As creative tools become democratized, graphic design
> will follow suit. I don't believe this means everyone inherits the
> talents of [iconic American designer] Lance Wyman overnight, but
> it does welcome a reconsideration of what is essentially a tool.
> Instagram Stories are graphic design. Type. Image. Emoji. Design
> can change the way our businesses are run, the way our world
> works and the companies we champion into our future. The sooner
> we appreciate that being a designer goes beyond the act of doing,
> into the act of thinking, the better design's position becomes.

Do you feel designers must expand their technology-based skill sets to stay relevant?

Diversification of skill set is probably more a contentious point now than ever before. You only need look to Twitter before stumbling on the heavily memed statement 'designers should learn to code.' For us, disciplines like motion, 3D, development, typography and industrial design are all tools that help to tell a narrative. Sometimes appropriate, sometimes less so. What I do feel passionately about is the irresponsible nature in which these phrases are touted to younger, impressionable creatives cutting their teeth. Becoming an author of relevant ideas lives beyond any medium.

In contrast, an awareness of the disciplines at your disposal absolutely has value. I can't animate particularly well, but I know how motion can aid brands in telling their story. Not everyone in our team can write code, but they do understand how to bring a brand to life in a digital context, be that native application or elsewhere. Every discipline is a vehicle for an idea or narrative. The former should be led by the latter.

Do you find creative clients to be more or less attentive than non-creative clients?

We are all creative to some level; it's in our chemical makeup as humans to progress, build and make. Sometimes we forget [this].

I'm not sure it's as clean-cut as saying one [client] well-versed in design would leave you to create more than another who is perhaps less so. Each relationship and collaboration is different. Sometimes we have to help our clients understand why we believe the decisions we have made are correct through logic and reason; other times this is implicitly understood. Some of our collaborators are concerned with typographic detail, and others with return on investment. This is ultimately the joy of building client relationships: finding the level on which to communicate and building the process around that. It's almost never the same twice.

Smets

by Coast

Based in Brussels, Belgium, and founded in 1999, Coast is a global creative agency with a heavy focus on branding – in particular, brand development and visual communication. Working for clients across multiple sectors such as fashion, finance, retail, telecommunications and music, Coast use a think tank-style approach to produce online and offline designs across a large range of outputs.

Smets is a luxury concept store that brings together fashion, design, art, food and drink. The family who created it opened their first boutique in Luxembourg in 1986 and since then have established another 26 locations in the country. In 2012 they decided to introduce the store to other areas of Europe, asking Coast to revitalize the Smets visual identity at the same time. Coast built the communication system for Smets using a solid strategic methodology, designing a bespoke typeface for the company along with an icon system that forms a base structure for signage and promotional materials.

To contrast with the concrete, almost Brutalist setting of many of the Smets stores, a bright colour palette was introduced into the identity and appears in every touchpoint the consumer interacts with. This runs through to the business cards Coast designed, with the utilization of abstract, cropped drips of spray paint, which feels progressive for a chain store's art direction. This aesthetic is indicative of the vibrant, fashion-led environments of the Smets concept stores, and by offsetting it with concise typography the desired tone comes across clearly. It feels high-end and refined, yet also appropriate for younger audiences, appealing to a wide demographic.

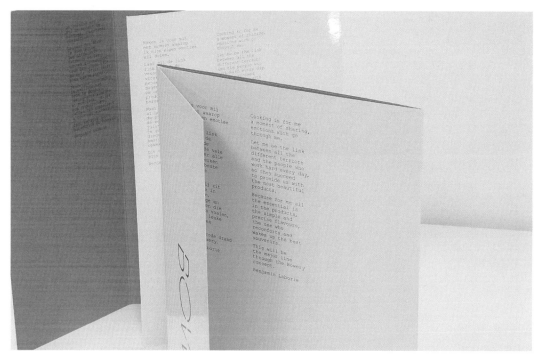

Bespoke

by DIA

DIA operates out of Brooklyn, New York, and positions itself as a design agency that specializes in kinetic brand experiences. Offering clients a complete package of branding and brand strategy, including motion and digital, DIA's method involves valuing end goals over trends and taste, ensuring egos don't cloud the design process. This clear ethos has enabled the agency to produce work for Samsung, Nissan, Discovery Channel and Nike, among others, as well as for a whole host of smaller creative clients.

To mark their tenth year in business as a boutique retouching company for the fashion industry, in 2017 Bespoke commissioned DIA to revamp their brand identity with the aim of appealing to a sophisticated, growing clientele. In such a competitive visual industry there was a desire to stand out from the pack yet also not alienate existing clients or stray too far from Bespoke's roots. The most striking element of the revitalized identity is the custom display typeface, which utilizes a number of weights and speaks volumes through its confident, monochromatic palette.

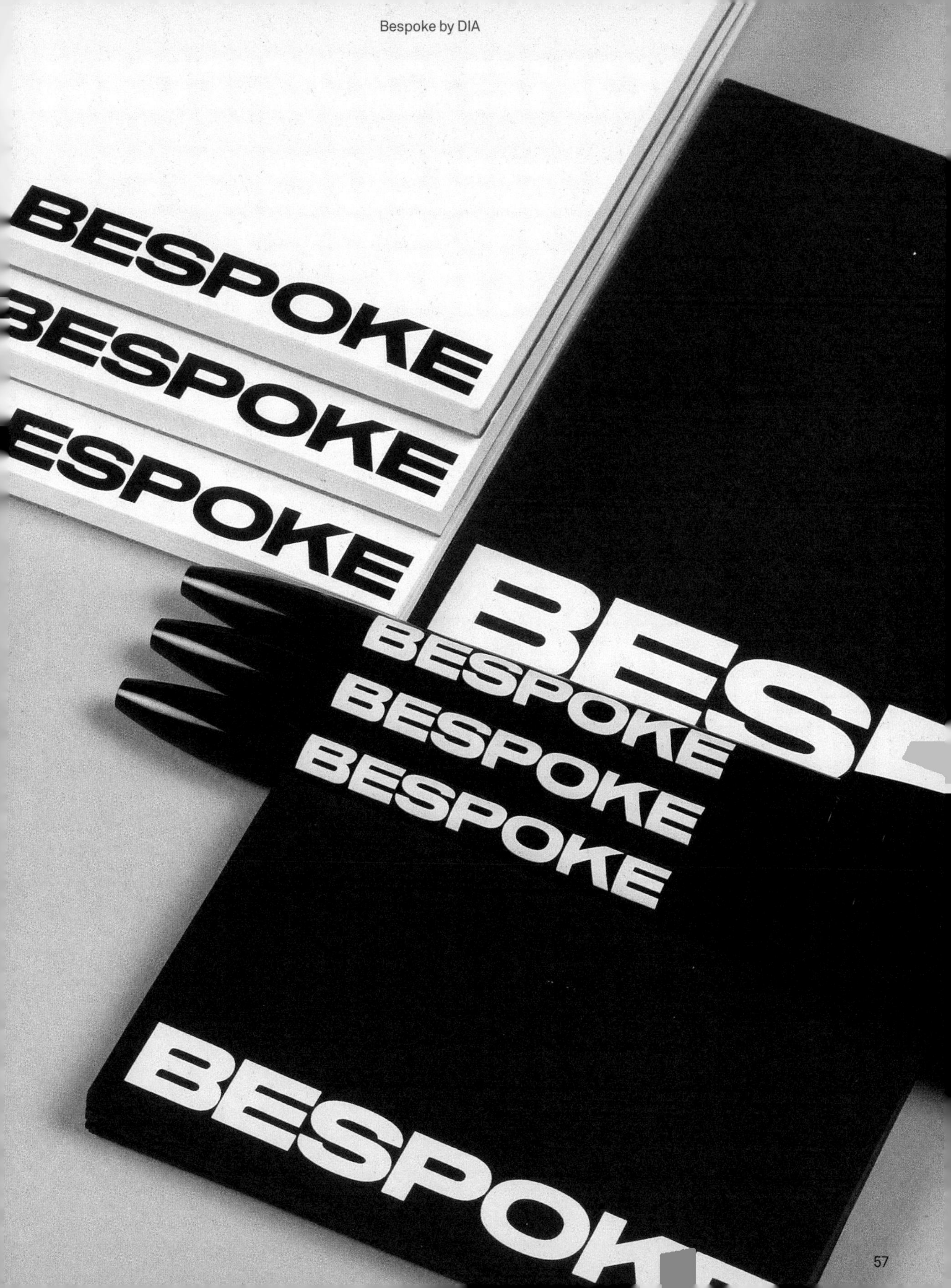
BESPOKE
BESPOKE
BESPOKE
BESPOKE
BESPOKE
BESPOKE
BESPOKE

BESPOKE CUSTOM I

ALPHA BRAVO 3 CHA
FOXTROT 1 GOLF HC
60 KILO LIMA MIKE N
PAPA QUEBEC ROME
UNIFORM VICTOR W
KEE ZULU THE SEX L
CHUCK IS A PROVOC
FOR MOST 'VERTEBI
MAJORS. 47' WE QUI
BLACK AXLE AND JU
GOING PAST HIM! 38
ENZO CALLED OFF H
MEXICO CITY JUST E
HIM THE CONQUISTA
WERE EXTINCT? 10.
FORM QUICK WALTZ
SIX BIG (JUICY) STEA
AS FIVE WORKMEN L
WILL MAJOR DOUGL
TAKE THIS TRUE-FAL
SOON? EBENEZER U

ACK

IE DELTA 8 ECHO
EL 47 INDIA JULIET
EMBER OSCAR
SIERRA TANGO
KEY XRAY YAN-
OF THE 2" WOOD-
IVE QUESTION
TE ZOOLOGY'
LY SEIZED THE
"SAVED IT" FROM
KIDDING—LOR-
TRIP TO VISIT
CAUSE THEY TOLD
OR MAIL.COM
EAVY BOXES PER-
& JIGS: 2,173
SIZZLED IN A PAN
T THE QUARRY.
BE EXPECTED TO
QUIZ VERY
XPECTEDLY BAG

Much of the output created for the brand allows the powerful imagery associated with Bespoke's day-to-day operations to take centre stage, with clearly designated areas where the type is used simply to communicate. The strong, impactful nature of the typeface runs the threat of outweighing the imagery, but its use is always well considered and balanced appropriately. That balance is enhanced when combined with the serif typeface that's used for all other text. Overall, DIA have devised a flexible design system for Bespoke that is distinctive in a crowded commercial environment.

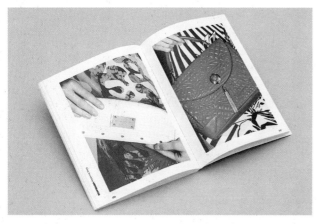

ABCDE
FGHIJKL
MNOP
QRSTUV
WXYZ

Arrels

by Hey

World-renowned Barcelona-based studio Hey was founded in 2007 and specializes in brand identity, editorial design and illustration. The studio's eclectic style often combines a mix of colour, geometry and bold typography and involves a holistic design process. Known within the industry and beyond for their side projects, including an online shop they opened in 2014, Hey like to experiment with new ideas and develop outside passions, which are then injected into work for clients. They've achieved great success with this approach, designing for the likes of PayPal, Transport for London, the *Wall Street Journal*, Apple and *Monocle*.

With their identity system for footwear brand Arrels, also based in Barcelona, Hey have hit the nail on the head in terms of communicating the company's slogan of 'upbeat shoes' visually. Everything about this design is optimistic and strikes a balance between the product's urban appearance and rural roots. The fact that Arrels's shoes are handmade yet mass-produced is reflected in the two colours of the identity and in the pattern created for the boxes and shoes, an idea also applied to their brochures.

The pattern's design stems from the idea that if one were to rip up all the layers of concrete that cover the urban landscape, one would find the natural surface of the earth underneath. This conceptual approach of torn-up, overlaid materials is abstract – but that's okay, as the majority of consumers see Arrels as an approachable, vibrant, authentic brand they can align themselves with. Overall, Hey's design system flows consistently through every touchpoint and helps place the brand comfortably among the mainstays in the footwear market segment, but also helps it find its own voice.

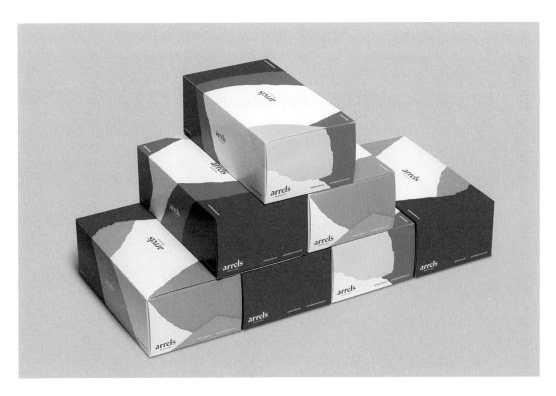

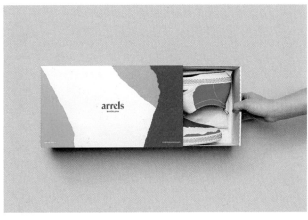

Nike

by Hort

Founded in Frankfurt by Eike König in 1994, Hort is one of the graphic design industry's most respected studios. Since relocating to Berlin in 2007, the team have continued to carve their own unique path by producing distinct design solutions across art direction, branding, consultancy, editorial and illustration for clients such as Adobe, IBM and Universal Music Group.

Hort's strong relationship with Nike started with external creative direction for its basketball division and developed into a now ten-year ongoing partnership with Nike teams in Amsterdam and Portland. Nike have clearly placed a great deal of trust in the studio, and it's for this reason that the output produced is so creative, experimental and often ground-breaking.

Hort now collaborate with Nike across different fields, including training, youth, football and basketball for the European and North American markets. What began with whole campaigns, events and product and retail designs has evolved to include a deeper role in the creative direction of the company, with Hort acting as a force guiding complex, long-term projects. Most recently, this took the form of a creative leadership workshop, defining visions of Nike brand design for the future.

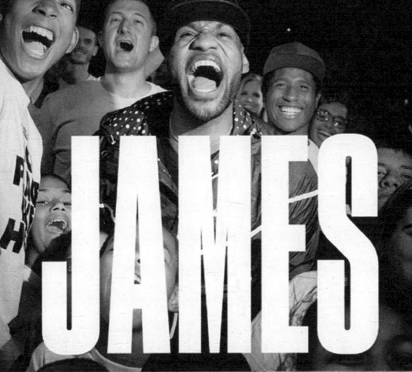

The Kyrie 3
✔ NIKE BASKETBALL

LEBRON JAMES

Coming full circle from this starting point with Nike Basketball, Hort also produced a campaign focused on LeBron James. The intent was to capture the roots of the sport through a series of designs that are urban in direction and fashion-centric, but often not utilizing the products as the main focal point – homing in more on James's personality and behaviours to evoke an emotional response. This direction is further emphasized through the environments in which the campaigns are placed as well as the techniques used to apply posters – rather than glossy and refined outdoor advertising, paste-ups are preferred. These stick out against concrete streets, reaching an audience at the grassroots level where the sport is played.

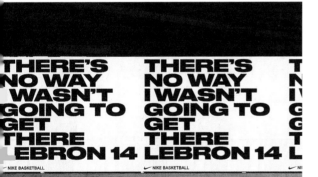

STÓR

by SocioDesign

SocioDesign is a London-based agency specializing in branding, packaging and digital. Its clients range from boutique start-ups to international businesses, such as space accountancy firm Stevenson Systems, chocolatiers Beau Cacao, spatial designers Curious Space and Nokia. By taking a minimalist approach, the designers at Socio help clients and their brands communicate clearly and efficiently.

To craft a visual identity for STÓR, Socio started by working around the menswear brand's existing logotype, which extends across all its products and packaging. Items such as underwear, socks and T-shirts made from sustainable bamboo and organic cotton are the centre of STÓR's offerings, and the design system Socio came up with clearly reflects this awareness of environmental considerations. The stripped-back, reductive design aligns with STÓR's style ethos and sits well with the brand's desire to combat hectic urban lifestyles by promoting simple living through their products.

The STÓR approach and the accompanying brand that Socio created will no doubt resonate well with the city-dwelling males who associate themselves with this kind of lifestyle. STÓR's slogan 'Staple goods for the conscious man' is given centre stage across the logo lockup as part of the flexible typographic and grid-based labelling system developed by the design studio. The suite of icons created to signify the products' technical properties and natural materials is further reinforced by the packaging design, which includes a bamboo plant illustration, recycled boxes, internal tissue wraps and unbleached card stock.

Boxpark

by Studio Makgill

The team at Studio Makgill, a Brighton-based design and branding studio, create memorable, clean work by focusing on their clients' most fundamental properties. This simple philosophy has led to the studio crafting design solutions for a wide-ranging list of entities that includes Nike, It's Nice That and H Furniture.

Studio Makgill's client Boxpark also operates under a simple premise: the world's first pop-up mall. Established in Shoreditch, in the heart of London's East End, in 2011, the site on which Boxpark now sits had been earmarked for future development. Using the space in a semi-permanent way by constructing retail units from shipping containers, Boxpark's founders created an environmentally friendly model and provided a way for both established and fledgling brands to reach large audiences. With a second location opening in Croydon in 2016, Boxpark has proved itself a mainstay in the east London shopping circuit and south London eating and drinking scene, attracting some of the world's biggest retailers and outlets to unique consumer areas. This is in part thanks to its successful visual identity, which feels like a super-cool, no-frills, out-of-the-box brand – an intentional decision meant to ensure their own logo doesn't take attention away from the brands and companies that occupy the Boxpark sites.

Type-heavy and with an understated, monochrome palette, the identity feels at home next to high-end fashion brands such as Calvin Klein and Lacoste, as well as younger, more up-and-coming companies. Arguably architectural in nature, the Boxpark logo communicates clear industrial qualities and appears as comfortable emblazoned on the side of a shipping container as it does next to this array of fashion-led outlets.

While Boxpark has grown over the years, its visual language has remained strong and relevant. It has aided in bringing in the city's hippest artists for exhibitions and getting worldwide attention for film screenings, and now with its second location in Croydon, Boxpark continues to integrate itself into London's consumer culture.

Interview with Hamish Makgill, creative director at Studio Makgill

Do you think that crossing multiple design disciplines is a viable approach to working within the industry today?

That's a good question. It's certainly something that Studio Makgill fully embraces as a philosophy, but is it viable? One of my design heroes is Bruno Munari, a gentle man with an ability to step between disciplines with complete ease – so much so that his visual range disoriented critics to the point where they struggled to write about him in any single cultural context. He was a painter, designer, poet, teacher, sculptor, author ... the list goes on.

We don't cross anything near as many disciplines as Munari did. We have worked on furniture projects and environments for shops, restaurants and exhibitions, but we keep graphic design as our core business. We are by nature curious and experimental and don't feel scared of exploring new disciplines, but we also appreciate where our greatest strengths are and choose to focus on them as much as we can.

Boxpark by Studio Makgill

79

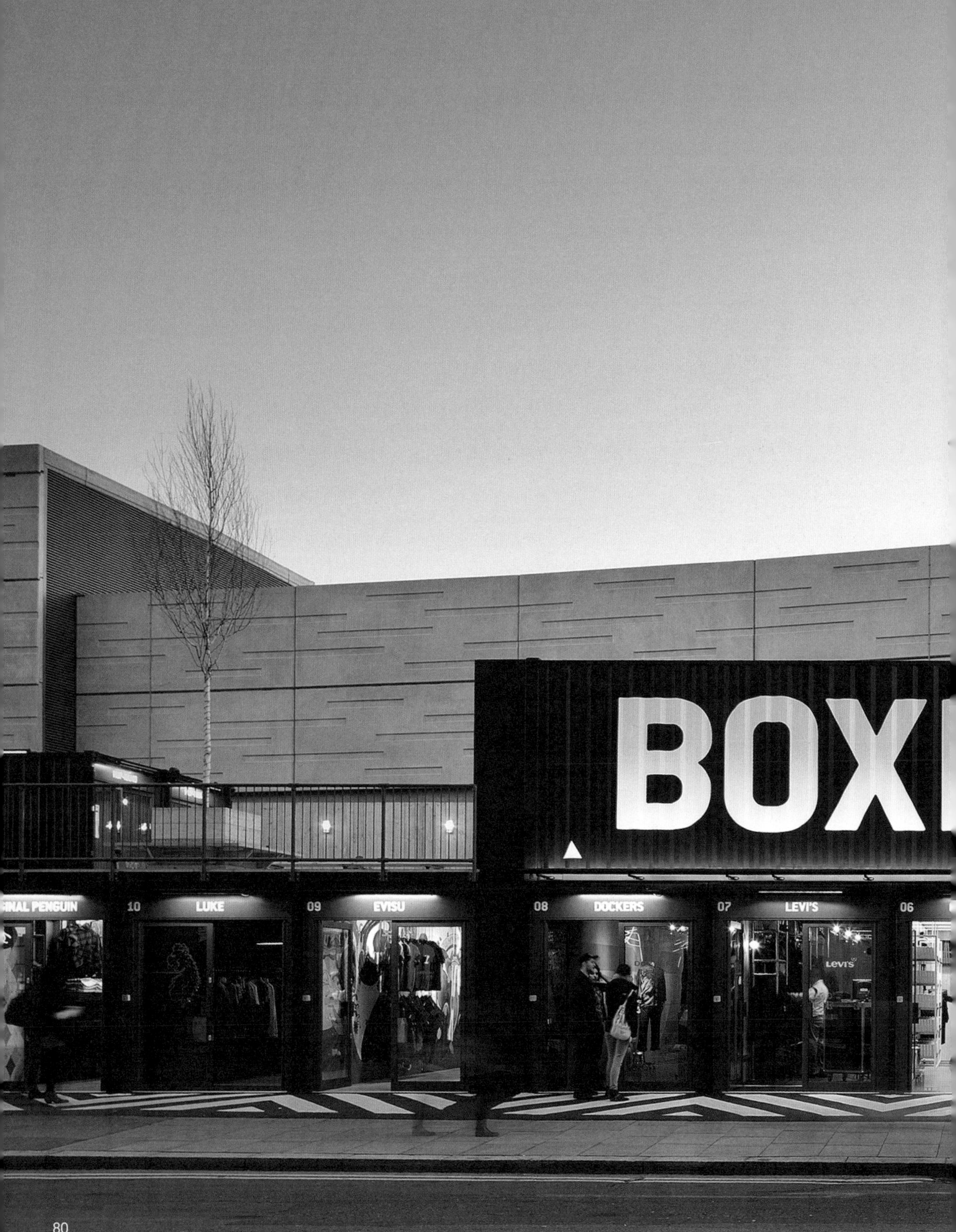
BOX
10
LUKE
09
EVISU
08
DOCKERS
07
LEVI'S
06

ARK
BS
BOXPARK.CO.UK
05
LACOSTE LIVE
LACOSTE LIVE
LACOSTE
LIVE
LACOSTE
LIVE
LACOSTE
LIVE

'We don't let the design industry
influence us (as much as possible –
we are, after all, visual people who
are constantly digesting what's
around us).'

Does your design process differ when you're dealing with a client
within the creative industries?

No, it doesn't. There are some differences when dealing with a
client in the creative industries and when dealing with other clients.
First, we already have a good understanding of the audience,
and second, we are dealing with a client who doesn't need to be
educated in the value of good design. However, we are still looking
to resolve the same questions: how do we help bring to life 'x'
product or service for 'x' consumer? So for us, our process remains
the same.

Every potential client now has access to software that can output
graphic design, in some form, at their fingertips. How has this
impacted the way we design for design-savvy clients?

I think if they are design-savvy, they will also appreciate that they
aren't designers. We rarely get any clients getting involved with our
work at this level.

Do you think clients are more likely to hire a studio or designer that
has won many awards?

Awards are so far off our radar. I see no great value in them. We have
won a few, but only because our clients have entered our work.

How much does the design industry influence design decisions
as part of the creative process when working with creatively
led clients?

We don't let the design industry influence us (as much as possible
– we are, after all, visual people who are constantly digesting what's
around us). We have a clear understanding of what we are needing
to communicate in each project and understand our audience. The
creativity that comes from this is original. If we discover one of our
solutions is not actually original, then it will be discarded. So, in that
sense, the design industry might influence the project.

'We have a clear understanding of
what we are needing to communicate
in each project and understand
our audience. The creativity that
comes from this is original.'

As a sector, film has traditionally been furnished with identities that move, too. Purveyors of graphic design haven't always had the skill sets that are more common today among animators and motion graphics specialists, which led to identities of the past often being lacklustre, with anything standout few and far between. Still now, at the beginning of even the biggest motion pictures there are questionable animated stings from associated production companies that lack the most basic graphic qualities. But, stings and logos aside, we live in a world where there is not always the option to have identities and designs applied to a touchpoint where motion is possible (this publication being one example). While the use of digital platforms is only growing, the recent renaissance of print and analogue platforms further solidifies the need for identities to function when static, too.

Momento Film

by Bedow

Perniclas Bedow set up his design studio in Stockholm, Sweden, in 2005, and it has since developed into one of the most exciting studios in the country. Working extensively in the cultural sector creating branding, packaging and publications, Bedow place an emphasis on having a sharp focus, often boiling everything down to one key word or phrase and then visualizing it graphically. This means that their output – for large clients such as Unicef through to smaller ones like the record label Pye Corner Audio – is a continual stream of well-conceived design solutions.

In 2015, independent documentary production company Momento Film asked Bedow to redesign their identity. Also based in Stockholm, Momento was founded in 2011 to produce short and feature-length non-fiction films looking at subjects from a less obvious angle. For this project, Bedow decided to home in on the phrase 'shifting perspective'. This is embodied in the design of the core logo through the use of a perspective grid, common in Renaissance paintings, which makes up the skeleton of the custom letterforms.

The result is an identity that feels uniquely ownable for Momento – it is considered, crafted and understated through its strict black and white palette. The consistently used black background has a cinematic, dramatic feel that lets accompanying full-colour visuals do the talking. The simplicity and uniqueness of the letterforms spark intrigue for viewers, who then need a couple of seconds longer to read it – but that's no bad thing. You're immersed in the logotype, as you might be immersed in a film.

3angrymen

by Build

Founded in 2001 by Michael C. Place (previously of renowned studio The Designers Republic), creative agency Build recently relocated from London to Leeds and is often looked upon as one the graphic design industry's most prized assets. Build bring a contemporary, thoughtful approach to their work, which spans graphic design, art direction, web design and typography for some of the world's biggest companies, such as Virgin America, Levi's and Getty Images.

Since its founding in 2006, production company 3angrymen has created films for the likes of Facebook, Manchester United, LinkedIn, Channel 4 and the Green Party. Most graphic designers would agree that printed elements add great depth to any brand identity, and while digitally led companies like 3angrymen usually have no need for bountiful amounts of ephemera, there is a purpose to be found along the way. Build devised a neat solution that employs multi-use A4 sheets that detail the type of correspondence and sender. It's a great way to keep print costs down, production values high and give a tactile vibe to a screen-based entity. The addition of perforation that doubles up to create packaging is a distinctive trait.

The design, while abstract in terms of art direction, boasts a clever bracket logo based on a screen, as well as a changeable pattern of slanted, hypercolour lines. There is a balance between these two brand assets that feels timelessly digital and clinical. The company's web presence aligns with the printed assets, giving a bold look and feel that's a welcome point of distinction from others within the sector.

[ ]LETTER
[ ]TREATMENT
[ ]QUOTE
[ ]SCRIPT
[ ]CALL SHEET
[ ]INVOICE
[●]CD/DVD
[ ]OTHER

'We have worked on a number of projects where the experience has been amazing – especially and only if there is mutual respect from and for all parties. It really makes people up their game.'

Interview with Michael C. Place,
creative director at Build

How important is graphic design to the wider design industry?

I actually think pretty much everyone in the wider design industry thinks they can do graphic design. How hard can it be, right? People do understand the value of good graphic design, they just think they can do it as well as a trained graphic designer. Graphic design can sometimes be a hard sell, unlike an architect, for example.
At the end of the process you have a building, you can walk through the door, go up the stairs – you have a very tangible thing. Graphic design deals with very complex problems, yet a lot of the time you might not get a tangible object you can physically hold. Especially with an identity, the most basic outcome being a logo: you'll get a colour palette, some typefaces and how all of the above go together – and I think some people really struggle with that.
I personally think it's mind-blowing the impact graphic design has on our lives. I just wish people would realize that and reward graphic designers accordingly.

Do you see defined professions within the design industry being
blurred by particular practitioners?

I think historically there have always been people who blur those
lines. I think it's a great thing. A good accolade is a 'shared vision' –
well, you can't get much more shared than that vision coming out of
a single person's mind, can you? There will always be super-smart
people; I for one applaud them. The flip side of the coin is the old
adage 'a little knowledge is a dangerous thing.'

Graphic designers often have to educate clients who aren't design-
savvy. How does this differ from working with other creatives?

It differs massively. Rather than slipping into the shallow end of
the pool you can just go right ahead and do a massive bomb into
the deep end. That shared knowledge means you get to the crux of
the problem much quicker, the process is much faster. But I think
that can come at a cost. I personally enjoy that 'educating' phase,
and just because the client isn't design-savvy it doesn't mean he or
she won't have a really interesting way of looking at the problem. I'd
rather be in a room of non-design-savvy people than a room full of
designers – it's much more fun and interesting.
    As long as there is a shared objective then I think
wonderful things can come of processes like this. We have worked
on a number of projects where the experience has been amazing
– especially and only if there is mutual respect from and for all
parties. It really makes people up their game.

Does working for creative clients provide a platform to push
boundaries that wouldn't normally be an option with more
traditional or corporate clients?

> Possibly. I think the reference points for creative clients can be
> shared, and that can lead to something ultimately less interesting.
> You might get to a certain point quicker with a creative client, but
> would it be more boundary-pushing? Not necessarily. By the very
> nature of the definition of the word 'corporate' – and definitely the
> first thought that springs to mind, boring, et cetera – you would
> think that would be the case. But then I would argue you aren't
> doing your job as a graphic designer. I find it much more rewarding
> making a great piece of work for a more 'corporate' client than for a
> so-called 'exciting' one. Where is the challenge in making something
> already exciting more exciting? Do your job: make it exciting,
> interesting, ground-breaking.

Do you find creative clients to be more or less attentive than
non-creative clients?

> Creative clients will always want to tinker or force a so-called
> 'informed' view. Non-creative clients tend to be more open to the
> possibilities of the project. I can't imagine a non-creative client
> saying, 'Can you change that Akzidenz-Grotesk to Atlas Grotesk?'

'I find it much more rewarding making a great piece of work for a more "corporate" client than for a so-called "exciting" one.'

FROM:
[ ] GUY
[ ] THOM
[ ] JAMES
[ ] SOMEONE
ELSE

Reel

by Richards Partners

Richards Partners is a creative agency in Auckland, New Zealand, working at the meeting point of design and strategy. Founded in the mid-1980s, the agency caters to both national and international clients, including construction companies, architecture practices, book publishers – even helping to reposition the public's perceptions of the kiwi fruit. To understand their clients' customers, the team at Richards Partners undergo an initial discovery stage, establishing where the clients are now and what they need to do next before moving on to design and implementation.

Reel was an Auckland-based digital content production company with a non-traditional take on storytelling. Started in 2011, the studio offered a wide range of services, from direction and post-production to distribution, animation and music (they have recently rebranded as Brewery). Reel's adopted mantra of 'formats change, the story doesn't' was intrinsic to Richards Partners' approach in designing the identity, which uses lost formats as its central theme.

Jacob Brown
Director
jacob.brown@
reel.productions
+ 64 21 075 3962

Reel.
Level 2 —
6 Kingdon Street
Newmarket
1023 Auckland

S–VHS.

BetaM

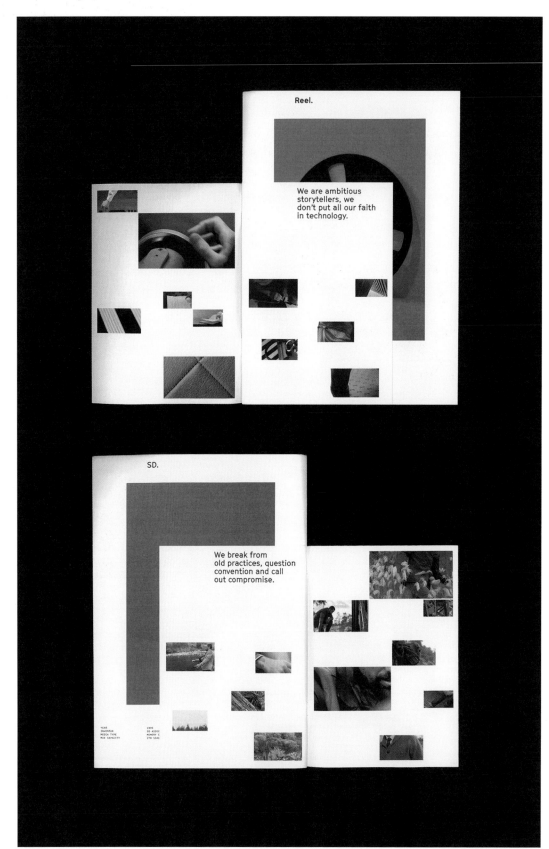

Simplified, icon-like imagery of VHS tapes, floppy discs, SD cards
and the like provokes reflection on the pace of the industry,
but makes a clear statement that the core craft of film-making
remains consistent no matter what advances in tech are released.
In creative disciplines, there is sometimes a tendency to allow
technology and new formats to dictate the final product, which
can lead to shallow and repetitive work. While Reel's work was
created with the digital generation in mind, the use of these
graphic elements communicates a true sense of authenticity. They
are memories of days gone by that trigger nostalgic responses,
encouraging clients to work alongside Reel to make new memories
for the next generation.

Storyline Studios

by Work in Progress

Founded in 2011 and based in Oslo, Norway, Work in Progress is a multidisciplinary studio that creates captivating design solutions based on conceptual thinking, attention to detail and careful levels of craft and finishing. Working across identity, art direction, brand strategy, packaging, print and digital, Work in Progress believe that good ideas should dictate a project's form and can be translated across many types of media. Their style is therefore as varied as their clients, and they often collaborate with other creatives, including photographers, film-makers, writers, artists, illustrators and product designers.

For Norway's largest film studio, Storyline, Work in Progress built an identity that reinforces people's perception of film as an escape from reality. This comes across through the powerful imagery at the heart of the brand's visuals. These photos spark intrigue as they are turned into abstract compositions through the coloured smoke clouds hovering within spacious landscapes. The logo's white square is meant to evoke a storyboard, encouraging the viewer to interact, which brings up a strong sense of ownership – one could, in theory, create one's own story in the blank space – all the while having a clear inspirational link to classic Hollywood aesthetics, which are reinforced by the script-style typography.

Interview with Torgeir Hjetland at
Work in Progress

Do you think that crossing multiple design disciplines is a viable approach to working within the industry today?

A design or a concept, an identity, can be implemented in so many ways and across so many different contextual surfaces. As a designer you are tempted to use those surfaces to communicate. You might end up creating design solutions way outside your expertise and comfort zone, but by doing just that you grow as a designer. You become more versatile and curious, even if it means making some serious mistakes along the way (speaking from my own experience!).

'A design or a concept, an identity, can be implemented in so many ways and across so many different contextual surfaces.'

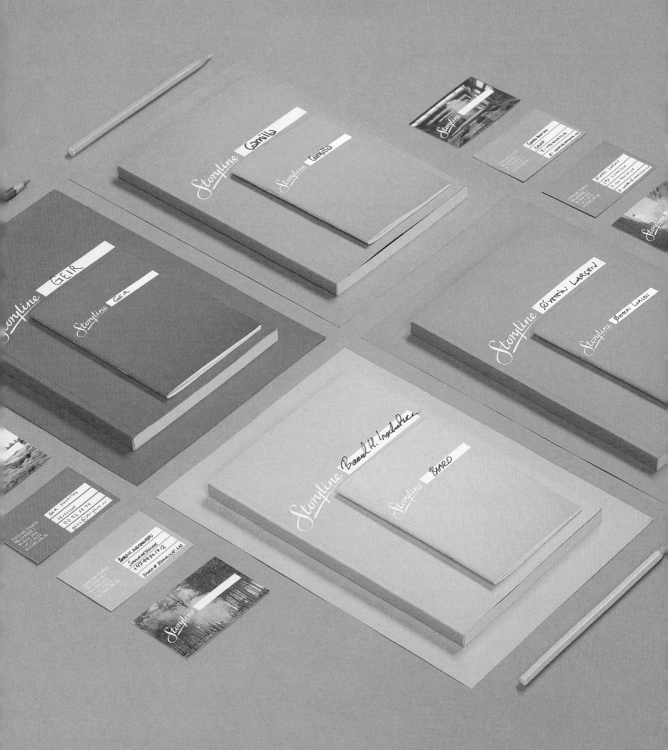

How much does a client's understanding of graphic design affect
the design process?

> I can only speak from my experience working in Norway, but in
> almost every project designers have to educate the client. Not only
> in the understanding of what design is, but also in the true meaning
> of design – its purpose, so to speak. But, saying that, I think graphic
> designers in particular also need to become better listeners. We
> have to understand the client and 'audience', not just listen with
> half an ear and interpret the client in a way we find visually
> intriguing as designers.

Do you find working with clients in the creative industries to be
easier or harder than working with non-creatives?

> If you have a good process, and the concept is based on the
> strategy, the client trusts the designer on how to interpret the
> concept. Then it doesn't matter if the client is a part of the creative
> industry or not. They all want to be surprised, in a good way, and
> challenged. It is all about storytelling, both in design work and with
> the final result.
>
>   In most cases other creatives choose to trust the
> designer. So the difference is not that big. It's a matter of building
> trust. Once you have established that, it becomes more of a
> cooperation, where both parties strive towards one common goal.

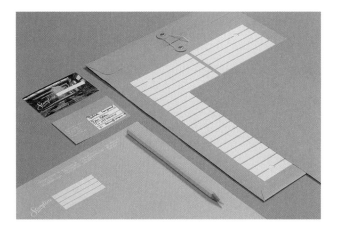

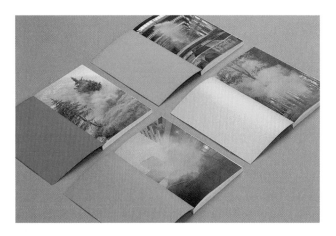

Every potential client now has access to software that can output graphic design, in some form, at their fingertips. How has this impacted the way we design for design-savvy clients?

I think we just have to work harder and adapt faster. There have always been big and small changes in society, and as designers we have to trust our skills and talent. If you are good at what you do, there will always be a demand.

'We just have to work harder and adapt faster. There have always been big and small changes in society, and as designers we have to trust our skills and talent.'

Do you think clients are more likely to hire a studio or designer that has won many awards?

In most cases, clients are not so interested in the awards won by the studio. The awards tend to be the industry patting themselves on the back. And that is great – we all need to feel appreciated, and another colleague telling you that your work is good feels great. In most cases, though, it doesn't bring you more clients.

If a graphic designer or studio aims to specialize in the creative industries, what is the best way to make that happen?

Some studios establish a very distinct style, and that can be attractive to clients, who choose to work with a specific studio or individual because of that style. How to establish that style is very much a matter of choice and coincidence. Some designers just do one project that creates a lot of attention, and suddenly a demand, while others have a kind of feel or look that separates them from the crowd. Sometimes it's intentional, other times it's more subconscious. If the client responds to a specific style, they have to make an active choice to respond in many cases to a style or visual that doesn't entirely fulfil the initial brief or the context. Also, if you choose a specific take on design, you are in danger of suddenly becoming just part of a crowd adopting that style or 'flavour'.

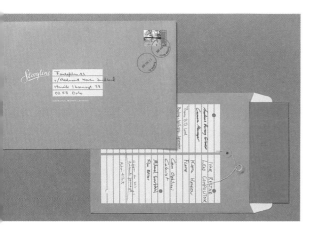

How much does the design industry influence design
decisions as part of the creative process when working with
creatively led clients?

Many designers and clients seem to surf the blogs nowadays.
Your work is much more easily exposed and spread. The downside
seems to be that a lot of the design trends seem to grow stronger,
and multiply in different forms, so the design scene becomes less
varied. It's like the rest of the world: there is a tendency towards
a global society with a few market leaders and brands, with less
individuality, which is a shame. I know I sound like an old man saying
this, but sometimes the Net creates less versatility because it is so
easily accessible.

How do you see graphic design's role in the wider creative
industries, traditionally and in the future?

It's difficult to predict. I hope future clients choose to use
the designer at a very early stage, when shaping a grand
idea or a product. Designers can be used to build business
solutions and products, not just give them identity, packaging
and marketing tools.

'I know I sound like an old man
saying this, but sometimes the Net
creates less versatility because
it is so easily accessible.'

STORYLINE STUDIOS
MØLLEPARKEN 4
NO-0459 OSLO
T:47 77 55 55
W:STORYLINE.NO

Helga Hoegh - Krohn
Produsent
T: +47 9014 1994
E: helga@storyline.no

STORYLINE STUDIOS
MØLLEPARKEN 4
NO-0459 OSLO
T:47 77 55 55
W:STORYLINE.NO

Knud Bjørne-Larsen
CEO / Adm. dir.
T: (+47) 90780996
E: knud@storyline.no

STORYLINE STUDIOS
MØLLEPARKEN 4
NO-0459 OSLO
T:47 77 55 55
W:STORYLINE.NO

Vidar Skauen
Jedi Master
T: +47 40 44 54 87
E: vidar@storyline.no

STORYLINE STUDIOS
MØLLEPARKEN 4
NO-0459 OSLO
T:47 77 55 55
W:STORYLINE.NO

Øystein Larsen
VFX Supervisor
T: +47 93245425
E: LARSEN@STORYLINE.NO

ARCHIT

Graphic designers tend to have a fascination with architecture. It almost feels like a level up from where we operate, since architects get to see their visions realized in the form of huge physical structures that jump off the earth. It's impressive, with buildings through the ages truly sights to behold. The graphic design world's associations with and links to architectural practice are intrinsic, from identities for new buildings and property developments (which are more and more common, as high-rise projects pop up across the world's major cities) through to wayfinding systems that rely on visual communication to guide visitors' paths.

ECTURE

This Brutal House

by Peter Chadwick

Operating under the slogan 'Brutalism + Modernism + More', This Brutal House exposed a new audience to architecture through a graphic design lens when it launched online in 2014. The project subsequently gained thousands of followers on social media, and a dedicated book, titled *This Brutal World*, was published in 2016.

Brutalism speaks especially strongly to a designer's graphic side – there's something about the straight lines and blockiness that resonates particularly well. This Brutal House celebrates the typically angular style by cataloguing some of the world's finest examples, with a solid balance of user-generated photography and original content shared via its popular Twitter account. The project was started by Peter Chadwick, the founder and creative director of London-based design studio Popular. He allows his own work as a graphic designer to inform his enthusiasm for and extensive knowledge of Brutalism. Chadwick has produced a series of prints for the project, too, which includes photographs and related graphic elements. With these in hand, designers can show their love and appreciation for Brutalism, modernism and post-war architecture – stylistically, there is something for everyone.

Interview with Peter Chadwick, founder of This Brutal House

Do you think that crossing multiple design disciplines is a viable approach to working within the industry today?

> Yes. Creatives with undoubted talents in a variety of disciplines will want to have opportunities to work in this way. The key to this is having clients that will accommodate this multidisciplinary approach. If you have the time and budget, this can always be achieved through self-generated work.

Does your design process differ when dealing with a client within the creative industries?

> No, I tend to follow a similar creative process with all my clients. At times I do need to be flexible with my approach, which can be reviewed after initial meetings with the client once their needs are ascertained.

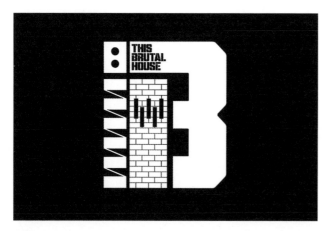
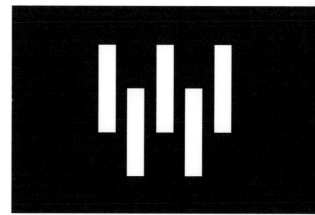

Gateshead   Trinity Square

Gateshead   Trinity Square

Gateshead   Trinity Square

Portsmouth   Tricorn Centre

Portsmouth   Tricorn Centre

Portsmouth   Tricorn Centre

London   Welbeck Street

London   Welbeck Street

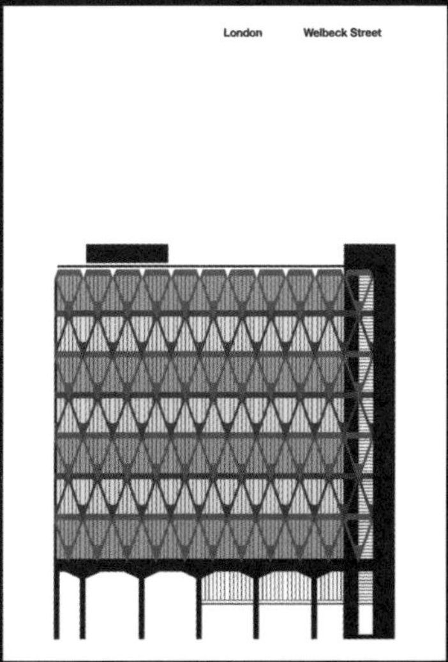

London   Welbeck Street

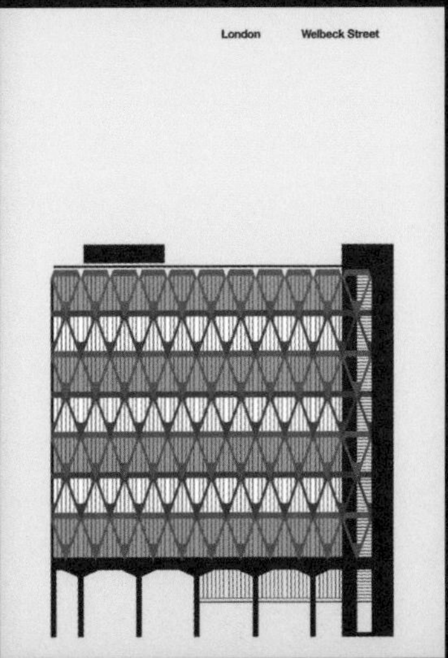

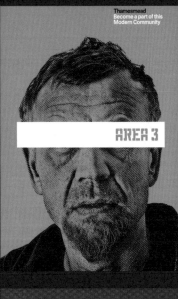

Thamesmead
Become a part of this
Modern Community

AREA 3

Thamesmead
Welcome to
the Community

The needs of its inhabitants are
being considered all the time
Thamesmead

Thamesmead   Varied arrangements for
Buying or Renting

The needs of a
Community that will
be considered the
best in years to come
Thamesmead

Forward Looking Both
PHYSICALLY & SPIRITUALLY

Thamesmead

Thamesmead   Facilities for Modern Living

Thamesmead
Advanced Health
Organisation

Thamesmead
The Town
of Tomorrow

Do clients in the creative industries often want to respond to
current trends in their respective fields?

People in general the world over react to ever-changing trends
and often align themselves with the hottest or coolest brands.
It is important for me as a designer to both acknowledge these
in the form of reference images and mood boards during design
development and then to look ahead in order to create something
that goes beyond a current passing trend.

More often than not at the start of the creative process
I ask my clients to put together a digital folder of images and
inspiration or a private Pinterest board. I tend to leave it open to
them with regards to what they want to include. From the outset
they then are involved and invested in the creative process. From
this I embark on my own lines of inquiry and research along with
my initial design ideas.

How much does a client's understanding of graphic design
affect the design process?

While working with a client with a knowledge of graphic design is
an undoubted bonus, it is not essential. I was taught early in my
career that it is important, where necessary, to educate and guide
my client through the creative process. In my experience, positive
outcomes tend to stem from honest and open dialogues from the
outset of a project. The design process will flourish when there is
a level of trust between client and designer.

The playing field should effectively be more level
when working with like-minded creatives. Not all collaborations
work, though many do. Through making more work and gaining
experience you increasingly become self-aware of what you want
from creatives when commissioning them. Beyond creative skills,
personality is also an important factor when you are looking
to work with someone. What is very important is to be able to
graciously accept when an idea created by another designer is
more appropriate for the design problem you are trying to solve.
The greater good of a project and the success of a team is more
important than personal victories.

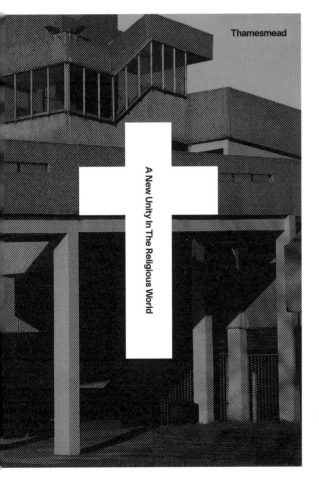

Thamesmead

A New Unity In The Religious World

'In my experience, positive outcomes
tend to stem from honest and open
dialogues from the outset of a project.'

Do you find working with clients in the creative industries to be
easier or harder than working with non-creatives?

> An increased pool of knowledge, if managed correctly, will not
> necessarily allow for an easier working method, but one that has
> the potential to deliver a richer and more varied set of outcomes.
> In a scenario like this I would say that project management and
> how the creative team communicates with each other is of
> utmost importance.

Does working for creative clients provide a platform to push
boundaries that wouldn't normally be an option with more
traditional or corporate clients?

> You are only as a good as your clients. If you have a strong and open
> working relationship with a client that is built on trust, you then
> have the platform to create ever more challenging and responsive
> work. This can happen in a range of sectors beyond the perceived
> creative clients. I see myself as providing a service that solves
> visual problems, and, when the opportunity arises, I question and
> challenge the brief.

Every potential client now has access to software that can
output graphic design, in some form, at their fingertips.
How has this impacted the way we design for
design-savvy clients?

> A competent use of available technology and software does not
> necessarily mean the desired creative response is achieved.
> A good understanding of software allied with the creative
> capabilities of an outside creative team who can objectively
> approach a brief often reaps greater rewards. This is not to say
> that in-house teams are not successful – the in-house teams
> at TV channels like MTV and Channel 4 consistently produce
> relevant and challenging work for their viewers.

Do you think clients are more likely to hire a studio or designer
that has won many awards?

Having never entered projects for awards, this is difficult to answer.
I would like to think that work produced is in the first instance a
creative response that answers the brief and hopefully challenges
the client to think beyond any pre-fixed notions of how the creative
will look and what it will say. Beyond this, the creative team, with
the support of a client, will no doubt be able to recognize the quality
of work being produced through to the finished outcome. A positive
response in the public domain will give further evidence to the
quality of the work produced and validate an entry into the yearly
design awards. Speaking for myself, recognition from the general
public beyond the design world is the highest form of praise. That
said, a Yellow Pencil would look great on my shelf.

How much does the design industry influence design
decisions as part of the creative process when working with
creatively led clients?

While it is important to be aware of the zeitgeist, trends come and
go very quickly. It is risky to rely visually on what is happening right
now. You should be looking ahead, be aware of now and delve into
successes of the past for new creative clues.

How do you see graphic design's role in the wider creative
industries, traditionally and in the future?

Increasingly, a graphic designer will be asked to answer even
more questions and solve more problems in order to deliver assets
for an ever-growing list of platforms and media. From the days
of the printed page to the digital age we now operate in, the
rigour and discipline of graphic design will continue to underpin
the creative challenge of delivering across print, screen, mobile
and beyond. I see the role of graphic design as one that needs to
consistently evolve while supplying solid foundations within a given
creative process.

'I see the role of graphic design as
one that needs to consistently evolve
while supplying solid foundations
within a given creative process.'

Thamesmead
A 21st Century Town

Thamesmead
**Catch a Glimpse
of The Future**

Fraher Architects

by Freytag Anderson

Freytag Anderson, based in Glasgow, is one of Scotland's leading design studios and works with clients around the world from the cultural, luxury and consumer goods sectors across branding, packaging and digital design. Rather than being tied to a specific philosophy, the studio treats each project individually, with a team being hand-picked according to what's needed for a given brief.

Freytag Anderson's identity for London-based firm Fraher Architects uses the visual language of architecture as its key concept. This is evident in the cornerstone of the identity, a floorplan-inspired 'F' logo. Simple, dynamic and responsive, it is universally adoptable across signage, business cards, stationery, the Web and more. The intersecting compartments create an ideal graphic device for containing text, images and textures. The shape and proportion of the logo can change, too, depending on the context in which it is being used (not unlike the way architecture itself is defined and restricted by areas of land). Rather than viewing the limitations of various formats as negative, here they are embraced and become integral to how the system works.

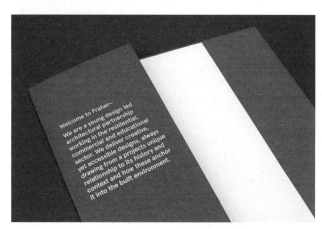

Fraher — Visual identity

Logo

Fraher Architects
Fraher.co

Line weight

Modular device

Linework

Icon

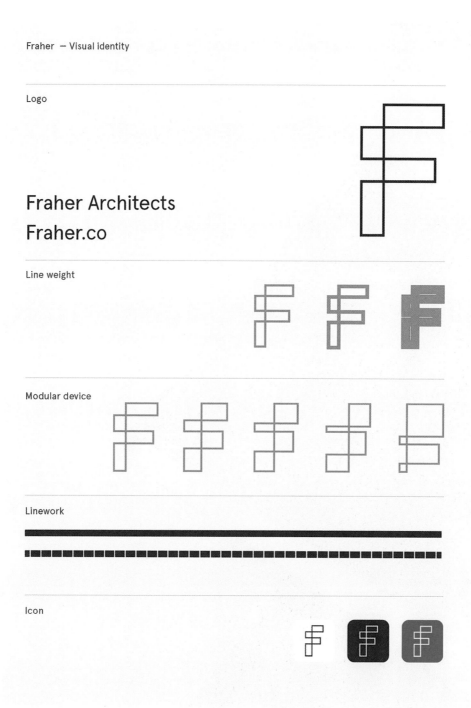

Fraher — Visual identity

Typeface

Apercu

ABCDEFGHIJKLMNOPQRSTUVWXYZ
abcdefghijklmnopqrstuvwxyz
0123456789

Apercu / Regular—
Lorem ipsum dolor sit amet, consectetur adipiscing elit.
Quisque iaculis nunc in ante ultricies, quis mattis lacus
condimentum. Ut ultrices scelerisque velit id laoreet.
Nullam consequat, dolor sit amet viverra pulvinar, lorem
massa rhoncus magna, eu luctus odio dolor nec arcu.

Colour palette

Warm grey	Scarlet	Neutral grey	Charcoal
C10/M7/Y10/K0	C0/M95/Y100/K0	C6/M5/Y4/K5	C62/M55/Y52/K28

Warm grey
C0/M0/Y0/K90

White
C0/M0/Y0/K90

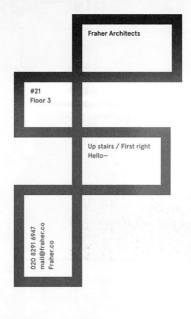

Fraher Architects

#21
Floor 3

Up stairs / First right
Hello—

020 8291 6947
mail@fraher.co
Fraher.co

The wider identity allows room for Fraher to grow and evolve as it moves into the future. The stripped-back, reductive nature is representative of the firm's carefully considered end products. Good graphic design is often said to be invisible, and Freytag Anderson's work for Fraher well and truly ticks that box via this minimal yet functional aesthetic.

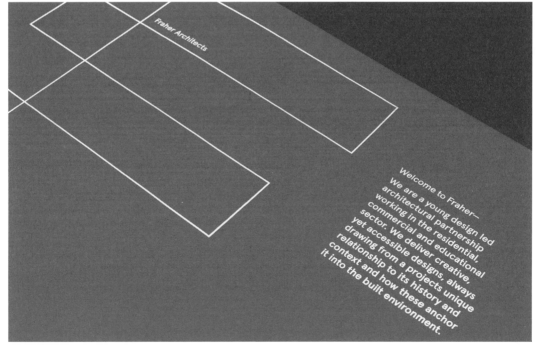

Rainer Schmidt Landscape Architects

by Hort

Berlin-based Hort (see page 68) work with a range of institutions and smaller clients, including landscape architect and urban planner Rainer Schmidt's namesake firm. In 2014, they developed a publication made up of six volumes for Schmidt. Titled *City by Landscape*, the project is devoted to the central themes of Schmidt's work, documenting around forty selected projects and including several essays. The individual 192-page books are Russian nesting doll-like variants of the B series of paper sizes, and the typography and layout composition are scaled proportionally to each format. The layering of the physical product's design echoes the basic principles of landscape architecture. Due to this experimental use of the printed medium, the respective interlocking formats can change and bring about different ways of thinking about the contents.

CIT Y
BY
L AN
DSC
AP E
BIRKHÄUSER
CITY BY LANDSCAPE
Die Landschaftsarchitektur von Rainer Schmidt
The Landscape Architecture of Rainer Schmidt
Thies Schröder (Hrsg./Ed.)
BIRKHÄUSER

CAMPEON
INFINEON
ECOLOGICAL
URBANISM

In Hachinger Tal, a valley near Munich, a campus for the high-tech company Infineon was planned. For this purpose, a consortium was formed of Rainer Schmidt and GTL Landscape Architects, Kassel. The challenging side to this project was to organise the layout of buildings and open spaces while rigorously conserving the ecological functions of the open space. Hachinger Tal is one of 14 green corridors protruding into the heart of Munich and facilitating air exchange between city and country.

The layout combines leisure and working spaces, suggesting that an intrinsically stable functional and ecological system fulfils a crucial task in a network of ecologic correlations and spatial interrelations. The "autarchy" of the company's headquarters in the heart of the landscape is vividly reflected in the compact arrangement of the buildings, surrounded like a castle complex by a circular pond.

The urban layout of the campus, designed for a 7,000-strong workforce, is as compact as a village. The extant green swathe was developed as a central open space framed by buildings. This open space, resembling t
the village greens, is meant to serve as a cit
The buildings' exterior landscaping is laid
extension to the working zones than as a foy
buildings. Firmly embedded within open sp
landscape, the project takes advantage of it
location.

Fitted between the office buildings, the inte
signed courtyard gardens may be used eith
areas or as open-air working spaces. Pits in
greens provide staff members with seclude
After all, facilities for impromptu communi
laxed atmosphere are vital to a campus pri
for research and development purposes. He
allocated to this use is much more than a "s
purpose of the campus as a field of commu
essential precondition for an efficient and c
environment, is crucially determined by lar
architecture.

Cafés, restaurants, small shops and a day c
installed to complement the working space
the premises, there are sports facilities suc
courts, football, beach volley grounds and
trails that may be used both by staff memb
of the neighbouring communities of Unter
Neubiberg.

86   87

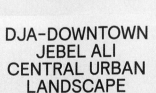

DJA-DOWNTOWN
JEBEL ALI
CENTRAL URBAN
LANDSCAPE

The Downtown Jebel Ali (DJA) project is designed for the creation of a new neighbourhood stretching for eleven kilometres along Dubai's main thoroughfare. A building by architects Murphy/Jahn, Chicago, has been proposed for the Central Plaza. This cube with an edge length of 133 metres harbours a vital traffic hub with an interchange station for regional and long-distance trains. While the long-distance train station is built underground, the regional train station runs on an elevated train path. The building ensures access to the different traffic routes, but it also accommodates a shopping mall, parking levels, and, in the upper storeys, offices, hotels, and apartments. The open spaces "anchor" this transit place within its environment.

The building is "carved out" to allow light to penetrate to
the complex's centre that grants access to the railway

The open space desig
it the key element of
and paths around it ar

The building itself is
street level, a number
quote themes of topo
of Dubai oases and g
planted patches revea
they safeguard the hu

Furnished with an an
leaf trees, the shoppi
central cylinder reser
spiral paths, visitors
scattered lounge area
the surrounding hustl

The layout takes up t
ons while offering w
their high-tech appea
and of paradise as pla
emblem of a certain v
structurally realised i

89

Laand

by Passport

Passport, a branding and print design studio based in Leeds, UK, was founded in 2012. The team are influenced by design culture across the globe (hence their name), and this is evident in a portfolio of work that spans the private and public sectors and both creative and non-creative clients. Their continued research into and experimentation with lesser-used materials and processes results in particularly nuanced and considered outcomes.

In 2013, Passport were called on to design an identity for landscape architecture studio Laand, also based in Leeds and known for creating sustainable, playful yet practical spaces. The identity's concept is based on contour lines, conjuring up the natural changes in elevation of the earth's surface and thus linking it directly to the field of landscape architecture.

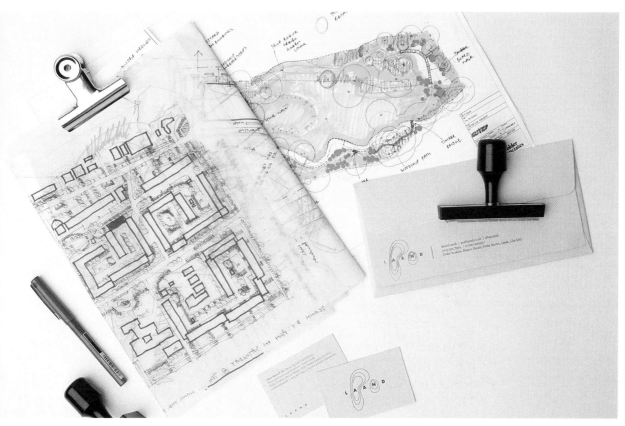

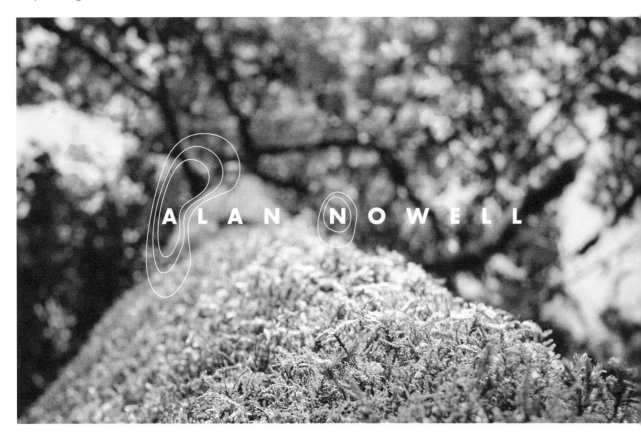

To provide contrast to the delicate, thin contour lines, Passport utilized strong, no-nonsense typography for the word 'Laand' itself. The chosen colour palette includes a soft, neutral grey, to avoid pigeonholing the firm, as well as a bright coral pink that sits nicely next to the range of green tones usually found in Laand's technical plans. Using a rubber stamp to print the logo onto various collateral materials provides a low-cost solution and also gives the project an air of authority, a sign-off that feels declarative yet friendly. An additional personalized touch is the rings around the letters 'A' and 'N' – a nod to Laand's founder Alan Nowell's initials. This subtle gesture provides an immediate anecdote for the client to tell as they pursue new business.

Primary Logos

Spacing

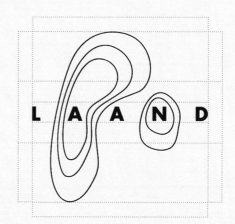

Sizing

Minimum print size
20mm wide

Minimum screen size
60px wide

Secondary Logo

Secondary Logo Sizing

L A A N D

L A A N D

Minimum print size
20mm wide

L A A N D

Minimum screen size
60px wide

Colour Palette

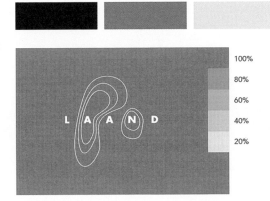

Pantone | 710 U
CMYK | 3, 76, 46, 0
RGB | 221, 74, 91

Pantone | 3245 U
CMYK | 51, 47, 49, 11
RGB | 74, 212, 191

Material Swatches

Typography

Aa **A B C D E F G H I J K L M N O P Q R S T U V W X Y Z a b c d e f g h i j l m n o p q r s t u v w x y z 0 1 2 3 4 5 6 7 8 9**

Futura Bold **LANDSCAPING**
Architects
experience

Aa A B C D E F G H I J K L M N O P Q R S T U V W X Y Z a b c d e f g h i j k l m n o p q r s t u v w x y z 0 1 2 3 4 5 6 7 8 9

Calendas Plus GRAVEL
Timber
brick

North Glasgow College

by Endpoint

Endpoint, founded in 1999, focus their efforts primarily on design for the built environment, whether that be through the devising of wayfinding systems or translating a brand experience to a physical space. With offices in London and Dubai, they have worked on a number of high-profile projects, ranging from Apple Stores and the Tate gallery to wayfinding signage for retail behemoths John Lewis and Selfridges & Co.

In 2009, Endpoint worked alongside architecture firm RMJM to create a wayfinding scheme for North Glasgow College (now Glasgow Kelvin College). The £20m building was erected as part of a project to regenerate the northern part of the city and went on to win a RIBA Award, with Endpoint's signage system to guide individuals around being the cherry on top.

As a contrast to the sharp, modern, glass-centric exterior of the facility, slender, hand-painted typography adorns the halls, emblazoned onto bare concrete, breeze block and plasterboard. Besides utilizing impressive scale for the unmissable floor-numbering system, a simple series of icons reinforces distinct areas and encourages exploration for people passing through.

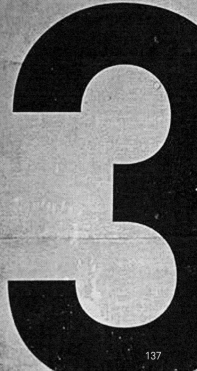

Does your design process differ when dealing with a client within
the creative industries?

> Our wayfinding process doesn't alter depending on the client sector
> or type. Our approach is user-centred rather than client-centred,
> as wayfinding design is about users. We try to set measurable
> goals with each project, and this can be easier if a client already
> understands the role and value of good design.

Does working for creative clients provide a platform to push
boundaries that wouldn't normally be an option with more
traditional or corporate clients?

> Creative clients are open to pushing boundaries and are usually
> more appreciative of the design process.

Do you find creative clients are more or less attentive than
non-creative clients?

> You can have both hands-on and hands-off clients regardless
> of their background. Some are more attuned to design and others
> are not.

Every potential client now has access to software that can output
graphic design, in some form, at their fingertips. How has this
impacted the way we design for design-savvy clients?

> The fact that design software is widely available doesn't mean
> that graphic designers aren't important, nor does it make our clients
> more or less design-savvy. Design software has altered the craft
> process and democratized it, but that doesn't detract from the
> skill of it.

How do we communicate graphic design's core value to creative clients when this is the case?

Our clients require experts in their field to crack issues through design. They usually are aware that they have some sort of a problem and know that it's likely to be something that they can't solve themselves. We push boundaries through the design process, we ask clients about their issues and why they think they have them, and we try to involve as many users as we can to understand user needs.

Do clients in the creative industries often want to respond to current trends in their respective fields?

Wayfinding is usually in place much longer than other graphic work; therefore, it has to feel right for longer. The trends clients talk about when it comes to wayfinding are around digital applications replacing static applications.

How do you see graphic design's role in the wider creative industries, traditionally and in the future?

It goes without saying that graphic design is a pivotal design discipline. It crosses many disciplines, from information design and wayfinding to packaging and branding, to name but a few. It's a core part of the industry that's recognized by most clients.

'We try to set measurable goals with each project, and this can be easier if a client already understands the role and value of good design.'

PHOTO

Arguably one of the most accessible forms of creativity, photography is a huge part of many people's everyday lives. Ongoing discussions about the ability for anybody to take a photograph on their smartphone and publish it to the world immediately is aligned with tropes about how everyone who owns a computer and a copy of Microsoft Word can produce graphic designs instantly. Yet even with these easily accessible tools and capabilities up for grabs, the work of professionals usually prevails. And when photographers and graphic designers collaborate, often relying on similar skill sets involving art direction, composition and balance, the creative potential of this kind of alliance is made only more evident.

GRAPHY

Hunger

by The Full Service

Twenty years after starting *Dazed & Confused* and ten years after the birth of *AnOther*, British photographer Rankin launched the biannual publication *Hunger* in 2011. The independently published magazine celebrates the new alongside the established and always highlights fascinating people, art, music and fashion. The magazine has evolved and expanded by collaborating with up-and-coming photographers, stylists and innovative minds who harness their creative drive to keep pushing culture forwards.

Since its inception, *Hunger* has gone through a number of art directional changes, which serves to complement the developing fashions highlighted in its content. By employing his own agency, The Full Service, founded in 2013, to craft its latest identity and overall design, Rankin has ensured that *Hunger* has avoided becoming stale. From creative development to brand strategy, The Full Service pride themselves on producing all their work in-house, delivering 360-degree campaigns for clients including Coco de Mer, French Connection, Versace and Rolls-Royce, outputting a wide range of content across film, still photography, digital, publishing and beyond.

By working with The Full Service, *Hunger* has struck a balance between being a fashion photography-led magazine and features-focused periodical. Varying topics are covered in every issue, which keeps content fresh and appealing for new audiences. Finding quality photographers to work with can be a difficult task for graphic designers, but with Rankin at the helm, *Hunger* adeptly curates a feast for the eyes across hundreds of pages. Well-considered layouts complement the accompanying imagery, displaying a true hunger for innovation.

Interview with Clara Goodger,
designer at The Full Service

Does your design process differ when you're dealing with a client within the creative industries?

Definitely: the design process becomes much more collaborative. When we curate each issue of *Hunger* we are often working alongside many other creative teams and clients – be it photographers, directors, models, stylists or fashion brands – on a 24/7 basis. Most other creatives tend to understand how the design process works, so they have their own personal ideas of how the visual output should look. Really it's an opportunity to craft an amalgamation of others' skills and produce something even more exciting than originally dreamed of. The boundaries are much more likely to be pushed.

On the other hand, working with corporate clients can make for a rewarding design process. They come to you because they've seen something they value in your visual approach, so usually you're given full creative control of a project, which for most agencies is the dream! Then it's just about gaining the client's trust and seeing how far they will let you push the creativity.

How important is graphic design to the wider design industry?

Graphic design is integral to the wider design industry. It all works hand in hand. It infiltrates everything, whether it's noticed or not, and should be utilized to support design as a whole. Graphic design has the beauty of being malleable – at times purposeful and functional, and other times simply generating a visual energy. When we design *Hunger*, the graphic design is fundamental for developing a sense of the publication's tone of voice, determining its identity among all the other fashion magazines on the shelves. It's my job to unite all the different design components that go into the magazine as one cohesive whole. You become very aware how the design will support the fashion photography, and try not to overshadow or conflict with it. When we have lots of different contributing photographers, all of whom have very different aesthetics, we aim to present the work in a way that is conscious of the original concept and style, but also takes into consideration the magazine as a whole.

Do you see defined professions within the design industry being blurred by particular practitioners?

At the moment, more and more people have the freedom to become multifaceted as designers. I think technology has increased the ways in which people define themselves creatively and it's impossible to not be involved. Artists and designers have to adapt to how people consume art and design and acknowledge that in the outcome. It's not enough anymore to just come at something from one angle. You really have to consider what the best platform should be for presenting your work, and that might be something you don't understand technically.

I've noticed the same DIY culture in the fashion industry, especially for younger people starting out – they have to expand their skills into all regions of design because they can't afford to have others do it for them. Starting your own magazine or collective means you shoot and art direct the fashion shoots yourselves, film them, create a website, put the material on social media, and curate, edit and design all the content yourself. It's great because the challenge keeps creativity alive. However, there is something to be said for learning as much as you can about your particular area of design and aiming to become the best you can be in it. There is a Japanese term, *shokunin*, which means 'craftsman' in both the technical and spiritual sense. It's about having a sense of responsibility to fulfil the requirement, and I think that's a really noble aspiration, because you can never stop learning.

'Design can sometimes become devalued by the thought that you are simply trying to make something look "pretty". A client may not understand that the decisions you made were for a very specific reason.'

How much does a client's understanding of graphic design affect
the design process?

I absolutely love it when clients have an appreciation for design!
Positive vibes right from the start. It makes the job so much more
enjoyable if you are working with a client who is excited by the
design process and values what you do.

Design can sometimes become devalued by the thought
that you are simply trying to make something look 'pretty'. A client
may not understand that the decisions you made were for a very
specific reason. Because design is a visual practice it can be
hard for people to look at it objectively. But as we know, there's so
much more to good design than that. There are layers of meaning
that we've come to understand over years and years of cultural
conditioning, and there's a responsibility to communicate this to
whoever your client is.

Do you find working with clients in the creative industries to be
easier or harder than working with non-creatives?

It really depends on the individual and how they work best. I'm
lucky because the team I work with at *Hunger* and The Full Service
is a rich culmination of individuals with unique perspectives and
outlooks, from practices spanning the whole industry. We each
understand the process it takes to get to the final outcome, so we
can be supportive of one another and remain open-minded when
it comes to collectively pushing outcomes to their absolute limit.

Of course, you can occasionally work with people
who believe their way is the only way of doing things and are
uncomfortable collaborating. It can be a very personal process,
as you have to go in prepared to put yourself on the line and have
your ideas rejected. But it's a really valuable skill to learn if you're
working in the creative industry. It's true when they say you're only
as strong as the team around you!

Maisie Cousins

L BE A FLORIST

"We're taught vulnerability equals weakness, but for me that has always been the other way around." Rosie Lowe's debut album, *Control*, and the EPs and singles that have preceded it, have all mined emotional and psychological disquiet in search of lyrical content and personal solace. Critical acclaim and millions of plays are almost collateral gains for an artist who makes music with necessary honesty. "I feel like I'm baring everything of myself. It's not an option for me to not be vulnerable. As soon as I'm feeling strongly about something this [music] is what I turn to."

One of the singles released ahead of *Control*, is "Woman", which, through its precise production and floating vocals, presents another cornerstone of Rosie's identity. "I'm an absolute feminist in what is a very male-dominated industry," she says as she introduces a track that has been defined by the music press as a quiet, post-pop anthem for twenty-first century femininity. "For me this is a song for young women, to say 'yeah, you're not imagining it, it's fucking tough out here.'" she adds, with "out here" stretching beyond the music industry and into the "male-

dominated, misogynistic society" that has forced women to its edges for so long. "Maybe this is a backlash to what has been part of our system for hundreds of years."

Control is an apt title for the album's collection of poised, composed tracks, though the project is evidently as much about release as it is about discipline: "I've been dealing with this topic quite a lot for the past few years. When you release an album, you can't control what happens after that. You just have to let it go."

And *Control* will be more open to interpretation than many records this year. The sparse production leaves a blank space between artist and audience that lends intrigue and – perhaps crucially in the age of disposable pop – longevity to an album that will form a vital part of the alt pop landscape in 2016. "I wanted this album to be honest and vulnerable and raw. This is my debut; now is my chance." So far, so good. ∎

'Control' is out now.

In five years' time... I will be 31... ho

Does working for creative clients provide a platform to push boundaries that wouldn't normally be an option with more traditional or corporate clients?

I believe that everyone is creative, and this is expressed in numerous ways. So even when a client is less traditionally creative, they can be very open to your suggestions and get on board with your concepts just as much as a creative client. It's a skill for everyone to learn to start trusting one another's creative visions and loosening the reins of control on the outcome. When you work with such an assortment of people, clients and your own team, you have to let yourself remain open to new directions and explorations. And that direction can also come from someone in a corporate background; it doesn't make the ideas any less creative or worthy.

Do you find creative clients to be more or less attentive than non-creative clients?

In my experience, corporate clients need to be talked through the working process so they can get a sense of how it all works. You have to communicate well and make sure they feel involved in the process too. But it's a two-way street, as they tend to bring forward some of the more pragmatic questions that are vital to an outcome's success – usually the things I would never consider myself!

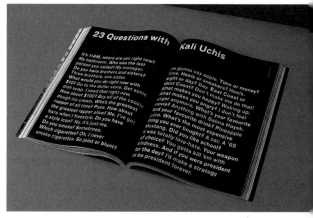

Design projects often get press attention in design circles, which helps to showcase creators in the industry. Can this also attract clients from outside industries?

It's definitely helpful for corporate clients who are less informed or involved in the design industry, because they can use this in some ways as an arbiter of taste. It's a gauge to understand who the key players in the industry are. But, to be honest, it's now working out that the more attention you can garner on social media, the more clients are interested. Design-wise this is something you just have to start catering for. How far will each campaign's reach stretch? If the public are liking, sharing and commenting on your work then that's extremely valuable to a client. I find it really exciting, as technology still has a sense of the unexplored – but it means you have to stay on top of things.

Do you have expertise or interests in other walks of design that have spawned due to working with clients in those fields?

Of course! To be a designer means you have to be curious about the world around you. It's a huge source of inspiration for me to see how other people work. Bruno Munari has a great motto to live by: 'Let us get used to looking at the world through the eyes of others.'

My job at The Full Service and *Hunger* only came to be because I was interested in Vicky Lawton's role there as creative director. She produces such rich and dynamic fashion imagery, so I asked if I could probe and question her about how to create more of this sort of work myself. Next thing I knew, I was working in the team as their designer. So it's always served me well to have an interest in other people's work; you just need to stay proactive.

There are similarities between certain design disciplines – for example, product design asks the same questions of balance and form as graphic design. Does this open opportunities for designers to practise different disciplines simultaneously?

I think you become aware of the skills required in different disciplines. Before working at *Hunger,* I didn't realize how much work went in to one fashion shoot. It's such a sum of parts: the editor, stylist, photographer, the model, et cetera. When I see a shoot in a magazine that's really striking and thought-provoking, I now understand how much work went into making it the absolute best it could be. So even if I'm not necessarily practising the skills myself, I can start to develop an understanding of what is involved and required in other people's disciplines. This has been a huge learning curve; it makes you much more tolerant and a better team member. That can only improve the quality of the design.

'To be a designer means you have to be curious about the world around you. It's a huge source of inspiration for me to see how other people work.'

Every potential client now has access to software that can output graphic design, in some form, at their fingertips. How has this impacted the way we design for design-savvy clients?

This is a common beast of a problem in the design industry, when access to Adobe Creative Suite then makes you 'design-savvy'! Undoubtedly it can only be a positive when a client has a knowledge of the design process, but clients having access to the software isn't understanding design. It can be nerve-wracking when you have to supply open artwork files for people to adjust themselves, because then you've essentially signed away all creative control. But generally the clients we work with come to us because they want to pay for the knowledge and ideas that we have, and they're invested in our creative process.

Ali Sharaf

by Mash Creative

Mark Bloom has formed a global reputation for his expertise within the realms of branding, identity and logo design. Based in London, his tenure as a designer under the pseudonym Mash Creative, formed in 2009, is known throughout the creative industries, with his portfolio boasting work for the likes of Beats by Dre, Coca-Cola and *Trace* magazine as well as a host of self-initiated posters and publications. He also currently serves as design director at SocioDesign (see page 74).

The identity he produced for Ali Sharaf, an award-winning Bahrain-based fashion photographer specializing in lifestyle imagery for adverts and editorials, centres around the concept of a letter 'A' rotated at 90 degrees counter-clockwise to create an icon of an eye. Having a 'good eye' in photography is considered a must for creating exceptional work; it involves much more than merely owning the necessary equipment. Highlighting this in such a simple way by relating it to Sharaf's first name via the icon is a skilful move by Mash. The coinciding art direction is conscious not to clash with the photography itself, but rather complements it when further typography is used within photos, alongside the photographer's full name.

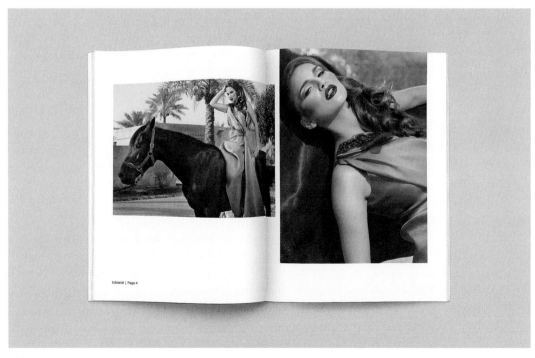

Shaima Al Mansoori | 2014

Makeup: Nadiaalblushi Makeup

Makeup: Ala Beauty Aalon

e Dark Cabaret, Harayer Magazine | 2012

Makeup: Leila Nasser | Hair: Waheeda Rawnaq

Michelle MUA Lella | 2013

Makeup: Masooma Makeup | Hair: Nea Matassaf

Grace Kelly, Harayer Magazine | 2012

e Cousin

Makeup:

Shaima Al Mansoori | 2014

Makeup: Nadiaalblushi Makeup

Alla Dashti | 2013

Makeup: Ala Beauty Aalon

Grace Ke

2014

Makeup: Waheeda Rawnac

It's About Making An Image, Tonne Goodman | 2013

Makeup: Azhar Hubail | Hair: Waheeda Rawnaq

Paper Girl, Harayer Magazine | 2012

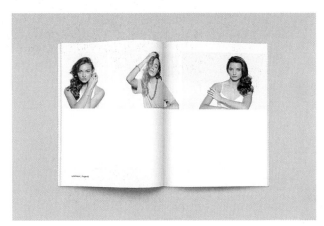

The format devised for Sharaf's portfolio is flexible and changeable as time moves on (as creative practitioners are constantly progressing). The system allows new slides to be inserted as and when necessary, with older work that is potentially not representative of the photographer anymore able to be substituted out. Throughout, use of the icon and surrounding typography is uncomplicated, acting as a subtle reminder of Sharaf's capabilities while letting his images do the talking.

David Rowland

by ico Design

London-based ico Design possesses a list of expertise that ranges from branding, digital, editorial and print to moving image, packaging and design for environments. Since the studio formed in 1994 it has amassed a client list that includes West Ham United, London Luton Airport, Benugo and the Crafts Council, along with a bounty of smaller clients across the world.

Even with photography being a hobby for many graphic designers, having a strong relationship with a photographer you trust and can call on for an array of job types is imperative. ico have found that in David Rowland, a frequent collaborator who has been practising for the best part of twenty years. The main feature of the identity ico designed for him in 2016 is the reversed 'D' at the end of a one-word logotype, derived from the simple concept of reflection and its relationship to light. Rowland has a knack for using light to manipulate the way his subjects appear, and this is a running theme throughout the printed collateral materials, as protagonists in human and object form alike take centre stage in full-bleed pages or peek from behind branded blocks, adding intrigue for the recipient. The identity allows the photography to speak for itself, enhancing the work through straightforward layouts while also extending to online and other ephemera.

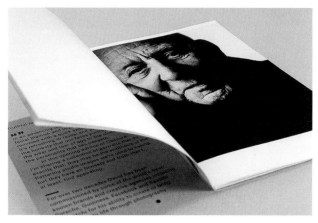

Truthful portraits

❝ ❞

In an advancing digital age where every facial blemish and imperfection are swiftly removed with a quick swipe of a digital brush, it's refreshing to reveal and even exaggerate the honesty that our faces portray; from the wear and tear of age to the clues to the personality that lies beneath.

In this opening edition of Obscura, I'm sharing a collection of portraits that do exactly that; they may be the antithesis of the flattering studio images we're used to seeing, but they have an honesty and truth that I, at least, find appealing.

For over two decades David has been commissioned by some of the world's best-known brands and creative agencies including Porsche, Guinness, Facebook and Saatchi & Saatchi for his ability to create or bring narratives to life through photography.

DAVIDROWLAND

+44 (0)7976 379563
info@davidrowland.photo
davidrowland.photo

FAO
Vivek Bathia
IcoDesign
75-77 Great Portland Street
W1W 7LR London

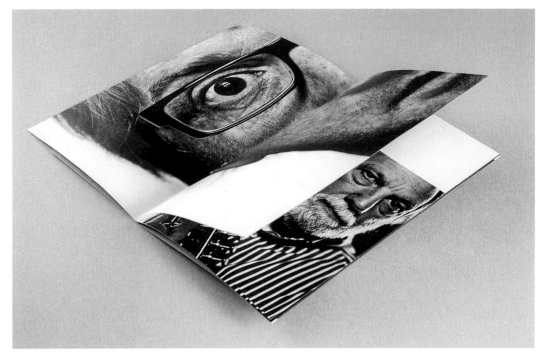

PRODUC

People use products every day. And because these interactions occur in such a visceral manner, human beings are well-positioned to make informed judgements on various items. For example, if a handheld object hasn't been put together with the correct surface material causing it to rub or create blisters, or if a suite of furniture has not been given the proper ergonomic considerations, you can bet that the buyer won't be happy and will be put off purchasing another product from that designer.

More so than in most disciplines, the want and need for a customer to purchase or use a product is defined by the product itself. But in this fast-paced, consumer-driven world, the graphic design and communication systems that surround products can have a profound effect on sales, too. Unlike in other creative sectors, more often than not, products are designed with consumer culture in mind; there is an inherent need to *sell* that product. This is where graphic design and the processes employed by graphic designers come into the fray. A designer might create a fantastic product, but without considered visuals and a clear messaging strategy, it may prove fruitless.

'DESIGN

Room Essentials

by Collins

With offices in New York and San Francisco, Collins's client roster looks like it has been compiled by a group of graphic designers who got together and listed their ideal companies to collaborate with: the Guggenheim Museum, Type Directors Club, Spotify, CNN, the New York Knicks, Motorola and more. Using an approach grounded in theory, the firm (founded in 2007) operates under a clear philosophy that focuses on the convergence of five key factors – brand, product, context, social and tech – to create seamless brand experiences.

Room Essentials, Target's line of modern home furnishings, called upon Collins to help boost sales and reposition the brand by making people excited about it once again. Research into millennials' needs and wants revealed their desire to recreate a visual world that they had seen on image-sharing and social media websites. However, their retail experiences in this endeavour were almost always in vain, culminating in costly or even fruitless shopping excursions.

This insight led Collins to frame Room Essentials as a homewares line that could make things easier for these young consumers. The products themselves already blended in well with reference images found online, so the photographs taken for the new identity system embody a Pinterest-like aesthetic, establishing a direct link between what's seen onscreen and what's found in-store and therefore encouraging a purchase. The consumer's journey was imperative for this new system to be successful, and by mapping it out carefully, the designers created a unified content-to-product relationship for the customer.

Does your design process differ when you're dealing with a client
within the creative industries?

I would say the process changes from client to client, regardless of
their industry. The broad strokes stay the same – listen, research,
develop a strategy, sketch concepts, edit, refine, present, refine
again, et cetera – but our approach varies greatly depending on the
type of project, the output and the type of client. As a very broad
answer that's probably more satisfying, clients in the creative
industry tend to be more exposed to work of this nature and are
often more willing to push the boundaries.

How important is graphic design to the wider design industry?

Graphic design as a discipline is more important than it's ever been.
The number of brands and amount of content people interact with
is greater today than in years past, and that content needs design
to make it meaningful, digestible, differentiated and beautiful. As
[American art director and designer] Paul Rand said, 'everything is
design', and that matters more now than ever before.

Do you see defined professions within the design industry being
blurred by particular practitioners?

I think the Internet has opened up a world of access and possibility.
What were once gated and guarded skill sets are now available to
anyone with an Internet connection and the initiative and patience
to teach themselves. To that extent, yes, there are people blending
professions in ways that they weren't just a few years ago. Is VR
considered industrial design, interface design, game design,
environmental design, film, storytelling or brand design? It's all of
those disciplines, happening at the same time.

But, it's a dance – design follows technology; technology
follows design. This process has been happening for ages, so in
that sense, no. Design has always been about blurring boundaries.
Eventually, what were once undefined, messy parts of the design
profession will be defined. By then there will be new territories
to blur.

How much does a client's understanding of graphic design affect
the design process?

Our approach may change a little, but it shouldn't have a drastic
impact. Clients with no design training often need some set-up to
ensure their assessment is objective and constructive rather than
subjective. That said, unless your audience are graphic designers
themselves, the idea should not require a knowledge of graphic
design to be potent. Everything else is just mechanics.

Do you find working with clients in the creative industries to be easier or harder than working with non-creatives?

Ostensibly one would think the former is true, but I find working relationships depend much more on the individuals than on where they come from or what industry they're in. I've had great clients who knew nothing about design and terrible clients who are themselves designers – and vice versa. As long as you build trust, I don't think it should matter.

I think designers are the ones who get hung up on nuances like typefaces, material, colours and finishes and other outputs. Most often I find if the client is excited about the larger vision, these details are rarely questioned. If I hire an architect to design and build me a house, I don't really care what nails he uses, as long as it works.

Does working for creative clients provide a platform to push boundaries that wouldn't normally be an option with more traditional or corporate clients?

Usually, yes. I think clients for whom creativity is a core component of their own business model tend to value creativity more. What pushes the boundaries for one client may be mainstream for another. It's all context. I think challenging work is usually a function of scale more than industry, though. The larger the audience, the more money on the line, the more risk-averse the client usually is – but, I've been surprised.

How much does the design industry influence design
decisions as part of the creative process when working with
creatively led clients?

I would say the 'design industry' can set the bar for what we – as
designers ourselves – judge to be 'good work' at any given time. Mix
that with a client who is more suggestible to those same values and
I think the design industry has a lot to answer for.

To be clearer: setting a standard is good. With the
Internet, access to design has exploded, and that has led to more
good work than ever before. But it has a dark side, too. If you're
overly responsive to the design domain, you will end up doing
lookalike work, and your own voice can get lost.

Do you have expertise or interests in other walks of design that have
spawned due to working with clients in those fields?

Of course. Through design my appreciation of visual art and the arts
in general has grown exponentially. Like most designers, I love type
and taught myself to make a typeface from scratch. I now know
increasing amounts of web development, user experience, print,
environmental design, photography, animation, et cetera. I think it's
an inevitable part of design and the curious minds it attracts.

'Setting a standard is good. With the Internet, access to design has exploded, and that has led to more good work than ever before.'

Every potential client now has access to software that can output
graphic design, in some form, at their fingertips. How has this
impacted the way we design for design-savvy clients?

Access does not equal skill. If anything, the increase in access
has flooded the market with substandard and imitation work.
Thankfully, design is also only partly technique. The true value of
graphic design is not just aesthetics, but insight and the creation
of meaning. There's no software for that – yet.

How do we communicate graphic design's core value to creative
clients when this is the case?

If they are design-savvy you shouldn't have to. If they are not, then it
becomes a discussion of intention, quality and experience. Effective
work is based on conceptual rigour, insight and thoughtful, unique
expression. Experience allows you to get to that solution faster,
better and with fewer hiccups. In the end, we can only advance
the influence of 'design' through the relationships and work of
designers. The benefits should be clear, or we haven't done our job.

DOIY

by Folch

Design studio Folch was founded in Barcelona, Spain, in 2004. Harnessing the power of strategic thinking, the designers create work within print design, naming, identity design, editorial and publishing, creative direction, web design, digital environments, art direction and photography. Their clients come from all walks of the creative industries and include *Metal* magazine, Barcelona Design Week, television station betevé, contemporary photography agency TAKE and lighting design company Marset.

In 2016, quirky product design firm DOIY, also based in Barcelona, asked Folch to revitalize all aspects of their branding and identity. This was timed to coincide with the launch of a new product line that introduced materials such as ceramics, porcelain, metal and wood. Attempting to appeal to a larger target market was a risky proposition that could have resulted in the loss of existing customers, but by enlisting a conceptual approach and executing top-level designs, Folch aptly achieved this. Taking Japanese culture as a central inspiration, with attention to detail, playfulness and production accuracy at the fore, the DOIY brand feels mature. This flows through to the lettering, which can appear in vertical, horizontal or square formations, both animated and static.

DOIY
2016
Fall / Winter Catalogue
2016
Fall / Winter Catalogue

The main typeface Folch chose for the project, Maax, gives
character as well as sophistication yet is also, crucially, legible.
The complementary font Typewriter, used for all descriptive texts,
provides a measured poise. The products made from less traditional
materials are offset by their display against stripped-back, minimal
sets, allowing the play of texture, perspective and hue to come
the fore.

Deciding to turn the idea of a product catalogue on its head, Folch
instead opted for an editorial-style publication that comes across
more like an art or design magazine. The packaging was the most
challenging aspect of the project, as it required the suppleness and
adaptability to be used across a wide range of formats and forms,
while achieving a certain level of elegance. Their solution ended up
successfully balancing visual appeal and cost concerns and helped
DOIY expand across a variety of markets, from design-focused retail
to larger chain stores.

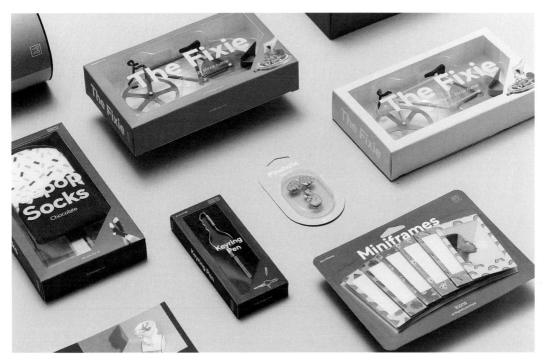

ByALEX

by Alex Swain

From his base in London, Alex Swain creates functional, minimal products for homes, offices and beyond. He's a designer in the truest sense of the word: after graduating with an MA in graphic design in 2006 and co-founding a consultancy focused on branding and digital shortly thereafter, he has exploited his overarching understanding of design principles and practices to work across a range of disciplines. His products focus on embodying a high level of craft and construction while achieving clean lines, functionality and beautiful detailing.

His wide span of interests drove Swain to devise a typographically inspired line of products, starting with his A Stool, based on the typeface Replica by Lineto. The letter 'A' has always had a relationship with engineering and architecture because of the purity of its form (and is sometimes jokingly referred to as 'an H designed by an architect'). This mix of influences saw the stool become an instant success when it was launched in 2011, popular within the design world while appealing to a mass market audience, too. It was also the first ever piece of 'carry-away' furniture offered by British retail giant John Lewis.

After sixteen years working within the creative industries, Swain is now a lead tutor of the London College of Communication's MA Typographic Media course as well a design consultant on branding projects and a product developer for retailers such as Made.com. Individuals like him are a shining example of the way designers can cross platforms and fields of expertise, making a success of this multifaceted approach.

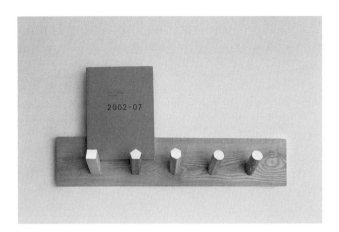

'The best outcomes are when the relationship between designer and client is harmonious and respectful – the role of the designer is to listen to the client's problems and then show confidence in the work they present.'

Interview with Alex Swain, director and founder of ByALEX

Does your design process differ when you're dealing with a client within the creative industries?

I would guess not. Over the years I've worked closely with clients from varying backgrounds, with scaling knowledge of design and the creative process. If you compare a very straight, corporate client whose exposure to design is limited and then, say, an architect, the process to responding to their brief is the same but the challenge lies in how you present the work. All design work is transient in that it can be developed and made better or more relevant, so when you propose the first drafts to a client with little understanding you have to make very clear how the design will function.

The worst outcomes arise when a client without enough understanding of design wants to have a strong opinion because they are 'the client'. The best outcomes are when the relationship between designer and client is harmonious and respectful – the role of the designer is to listen to the client's problems and then show confidence in the work they present. If you show any doubt in your own work, the client relationship can shatter.

How important is graphic design to the wider design industry?

Very, as it is probably the most commonly studied design discipline. I've met so many friends over the years who studied graphic design and have developed into interactive designers, film-makers or motion graphics designers. Not to sound grumpy, but the democratization of design through more access to creative software has led to everyone thinking they are a designer. You decide if that's a good thing or not!

Do you find working with clients in the creative industries to be easier or harder than working with non-creatives?

It depends on the personalities in the group. All projects need leaders, thinkers and doers ... it's a design food chain, and any creative collaboration needs to have clear roles and responsibilities for each party. Just because a team all understands design, it doesn't mean the ideas are any better – maybe they are realized quicker? Good design needs hard work and a defined brief to be judged against; that's all that matters to me.

Does working for creative clients provide a platform to push boundaries that wouldn't normally be an option with more traditional or corporate clients?

> No, I really believe the boundaries are pushed when the client– designer relationship is respectful. If you have the same ambitions for the work, great ideas will follow.

There are similarities between certain design disciplines – for example, product design asks the same questions of balance and form as graphic design. Does this open opportunities for designers to practise different disciplines simultaneously?

> Yes. I think more graphic designers should cross over to product design, as each discipline will improve the other. We all need to stimulate our 'ideas', and working across disciplines is a great way to see things differently. I started a furniture brand because I was sick of the mostly digital design briefs we had coming through our studio at the time. I missed the physicality of design and working with texture, materials and finishes that print work used to offer. My interests in typography and a minimal approach to design come through in the furniture ideas. It took a long time to build the confidence that I could design and make serious furniture again and again. I think this was helped slightly by the fact I've always felt like a graphic designer fraud – so why not be a product designer fraud too!

'We all need to stimulate our "ideas", and working across disciplines is a great way to see things differently.'

Finchtail

by Believe in®

Believe in® is a creative studio founded in 1996, with offices in Exeter, UK, and Ontario, Canada. Their work is process-driven, achieved through the application of a classic four-dimensional design framework of 'Discover, Define, Develop and Deliver' to all projects the team are involved in. They design for brands across print, digital, packaging and environments, and clients range from Falmouth University, Coca-Cola and Uproot maple syrup to type foundry Fontsmith and *Icon* magazine.

Finchtail, a product design company dedicated to making simple, useful, sustainable objects, launched in 2014. The firm brought in Believe in® to assist with identity and packaging, and every aspect of the brand experience created by the studio reflects Finchtail's ethos. The triangular marque is inspired by their first offerings – cardboard stands for tablets and smartphones – while also conjuring up the ideas of portability and outdoor adventure. Bright orange card stock – recalling the plumage of finches – is set against neutral and naturally evocative paperboard, while text is restricted to the simplicity of black and white. The visual language complements the tone of voice throughout the entirety of the communications, bringing a further sense of humanity and simplicity that reinforces the brand ethos, only working to enhance the experience for the customer.

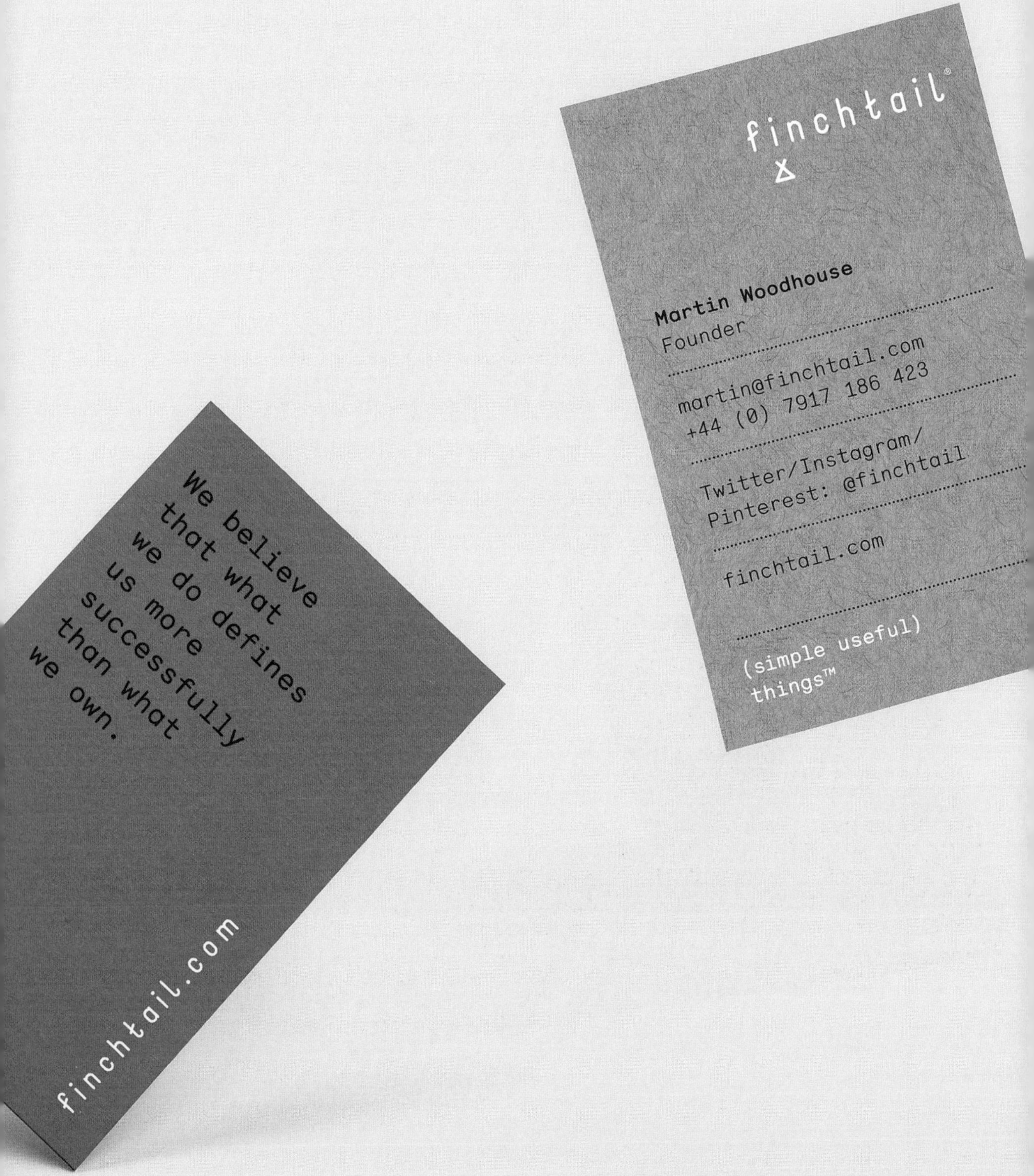

finchtail®
∆

Martin Woodhouse
Founder

martin@finchtail.com
+44 (0) 7917 186 423

Twitter/Instagram/
Pinterest: @finchtail

finchtail.com

(simple useful)
things™

We believe
that what
we do defines
us more
successfully
than what
we own.

finchtail.com

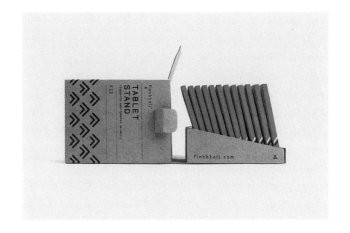

The contrast between Finchtail's stripped-back, rustic products, which feature art direction indicative of a time gone by, and the ultra-modern machines they are designed to hold is notable; it's this juxtaposition that serves the end result so well. And, while the tablets and smartphones these products were built for could be looked upon as cold and robotic, they are designed by and for humans, too. The identity succeeds because it reflects this dual character.

Bec Brittain

by Lotta Nieminen

Helsinki-born, New York-based Lotta Nieminen has had an illustrious career to date, working at iconic studios Pentagram and RoAndCo before setting up her own practice, receiving an Art Directors Club Young Guns award in 2010 and being nominated for *Forbes* magazine's annual 30 Under 30 list in the Art and Style category in 2014. Google, Volkswagen, the *New York Times*, IBM, *Wired* and United Airlines pepper her client list, which is also populated by smaller creative entities, all of whom she collaborates with on graphic design, illustration and art direction.

Nieminen's oeuvre appears to tend towards the classic and refined. While her use of typography is often very stripped back, it achieves a level of personality and flair that enables it to sit comfortably next to diverse examples of art direction and product photography. The visual identity she devised for Bec Brittain is a harmonious continuation of the New York-based lighting and product designer's output: contemporary and elevated. Taking inspiration from the combination of materials and handicraft used to produce Brittain's lighting, the logo comprises two different typefaces. Business cards and a related catalogue utilize dark surfaces finished with a foiled version of the logo that almost glows, reminiscent of LED lights. They are beautiful items in and of themselves that encourage the products to be sold, with an essence of quality echoed through the layouts, format and printing specifications.

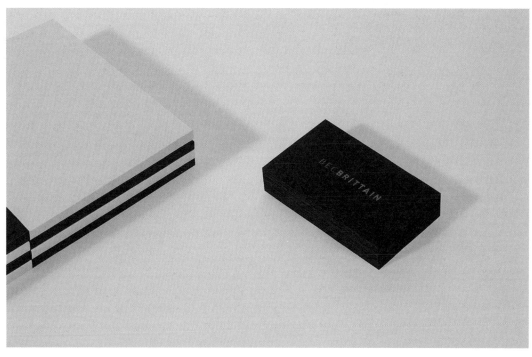

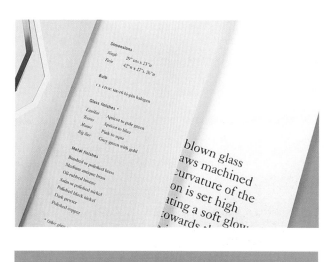

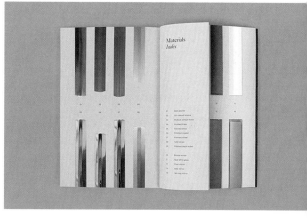

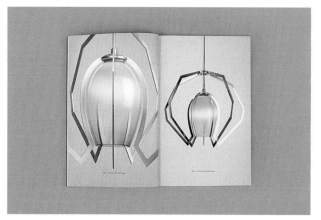

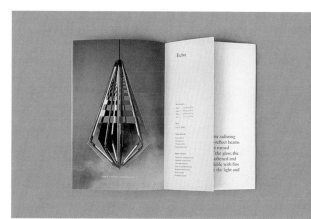

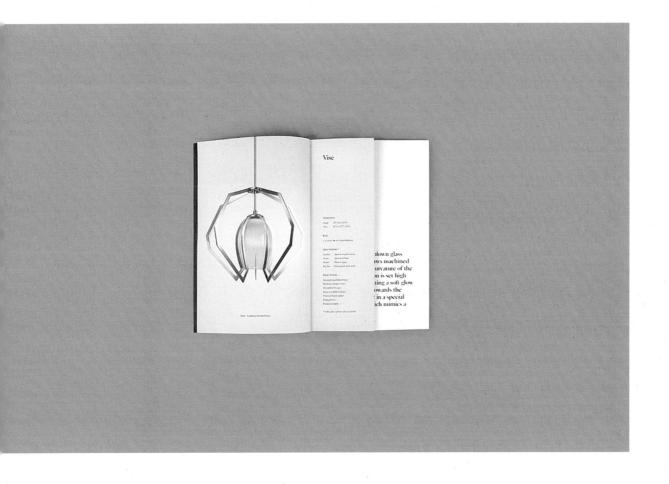

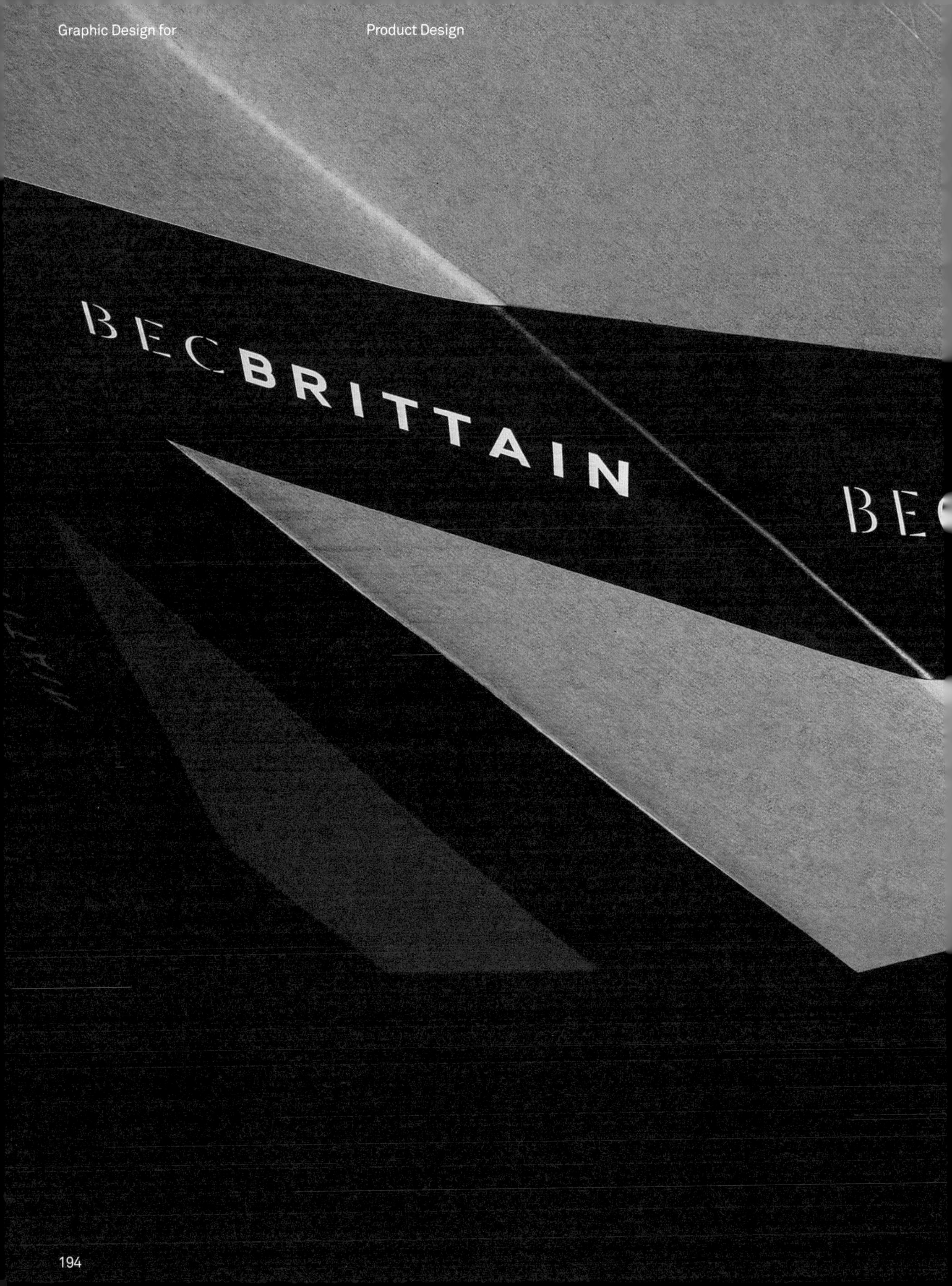
BECBRITTAIN
BEC

This is what branding is all about: for many potential customers, these photos of printed assets will be the first interaction with the brand online, showing how important well-considered design elements can be. Sometimes, graphic communications surrounding products can eclipse the products themselves, but Nieminen's subtle ideas do a great job of letting Brittain's work breathe.

EVERYTHING

13

The creative industries as a whole are a large entity, appealing inwardly and outwardly to a vast number of stakeholders who have differing agendas in regard to how they interact with the fields in question and consume products and ideas. Naturally, designers who claim to be invested in the cultural sector get their hands dirty by working for it and immersing themselves in it, both professionally and personally. With that in mind, this final chapter aims to encapsulate a list of projects that don't fall into any of the previous categories, but still show exemplary use of graphic design, from event spaces to theatres to premium paper suppliers and beyond.

IN BETWEEN

Printworks

by Only

Only was founded in 2014 and recently moved offices from Leeds to Manchester. The studio has worked with an impressive list of clients, including Aston Martin, Goldsmiths, University of London, the British Interactive Media Association, Honda and the University of Suffolk, across branding, print and digital. Consulting on strategy and design is at the heart of what Only do; the team put their skills to use in helping companies and organizations flourish.

Aiming to add a dose of innovation to London's culture scene, Printworks opened in 2016, comprising six event spaces on the 16-acre site of a former printing factory. Immediately, it became a beacon for music, theatre, film, fashion and more in the capital. The identity Only created to mark the venue's launch drew directly from its history, designing a logotype inspired by a printing press's rollers. Digitally 'wrapping' the typography around a cylindrical form allows a virtually infinite range of variations of the client name to be generated. This simple, strong concept is careful not to lean too far towards any one creative discipline that takes place within the venue's walls, remaining neutral yet displaying a distinct personality. The extended art direction, driven by typography (specifically, the Druk font family), functions in much the same way – it can sit confidently on its own but equally can be used to support and enhance related imagery, posters, online ephemera and so on.

For an organization such as Printworks that is putting on cutting-edge events, it is important to keep on top of (and even ahead of) current trends; the space must stay in the vanguard of cultural activity to thrive. The bold, confident communications system Only have created employs a visual language that is so strong, it will no doubt endure into the future.

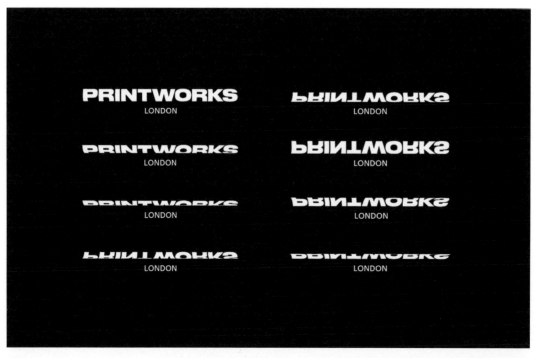

MENU   SUBSCRIBE

NTS   EVE

04 FEB

SATURDAY 04 FEB
9.30PM–3AM
FROM £25

Seth Troxler
Martinez Brothers
Loco Dice
Michael Mayer
Andhim
Netsky

MENU   SUBSCRI

LE SAC
PRINTE

SATURDAY 27 FEB
12.00PM–8.00PM

£37.50

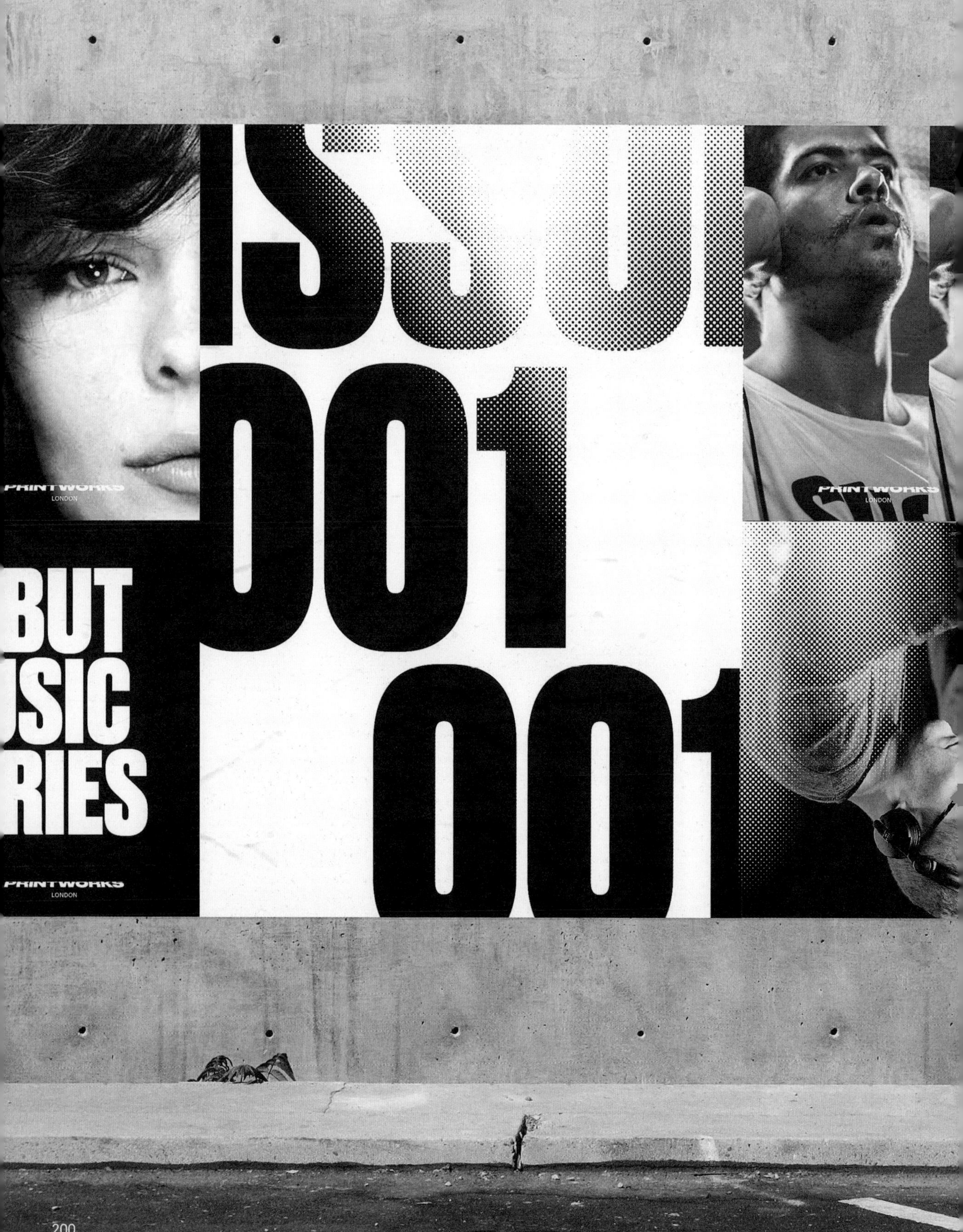
SSU
001
PRINTWORKS
LONDON
PRINTWORKS
LONDON
001
BUT
JSIC
RIES
PRINTWORKS
LONDON

& STATUS
CHAS...
RTINEZ
THE MART...EZ
ERS
BROTHERS
ICE
LOCO DICE
RAVIZ
NINA KRAVIZ
CUS
SUB FOCUS
EYER
ADAM BEYER
DAPHNI

ISSU

PRINTWORKS LONDON

001

PRINTWORKS LONDON

PRINTWORKS LONDON

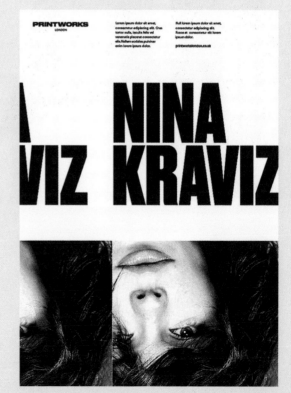

17

DAPHNI
JOY ORBISON
FLOATING POINTS
& HUNEE

Lorem ipsum dolor sit amet, consectetur adipiscing elit. Cras tortor nulla, iaculis felis vel venenatis placerat consectetur eis nisbem. Lorem ipsum dolor sit amet, consectetur adipiscing elit. Cras tortor nulla, Lorem ipsum dolor sit amet, conse ctetur adipiscing elit.

Lorem ipsum dolor sit amet, consectetur adipiscing elit. Fusce et sodales erotolos eget fringilla. Lorem ipsum dolor sit amet, consectetur adipiscing elit. Cras tortor nulla, iaculis.

Visit
Printworkslondon.co.uk

PRINTWORKS
LONDON

FEB

CHASE & STATUS
KEVIN OVER
LOCO DICE
THE MARTINEZ BROTHERS
SETH TROXLER
WILLIAM DJOKO
KRANKBROTHER
GEDDES
G WALKER
ALAN FITZPATRICK
MAX COOPER

PRINTWORKS
LONDON

ISSUE 001

CHASE & STATUS
SETH TROXLER B2B
LOCO DICE B2B
THE MARTINEZ BROTHERS
WILLIAM DJOKO
KRANKBROTHER
GEDDES
G WALKER
JOEL MULL
KEVIN OVER

PRINTWORKS
LONDON

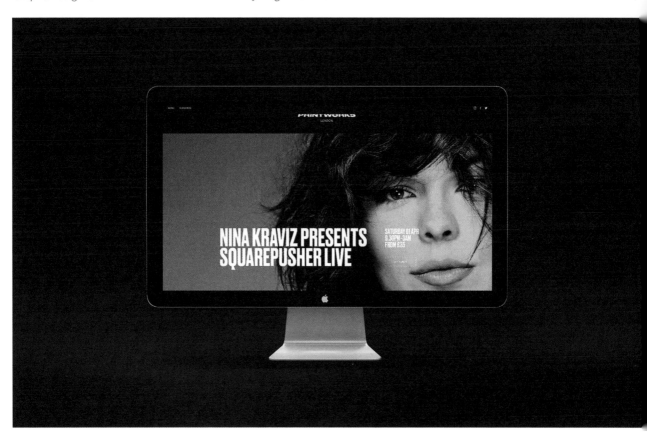

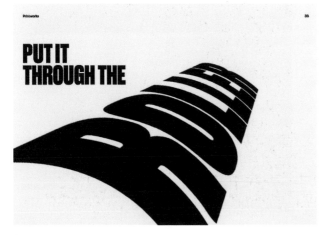

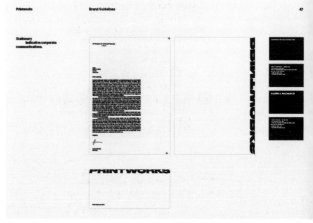

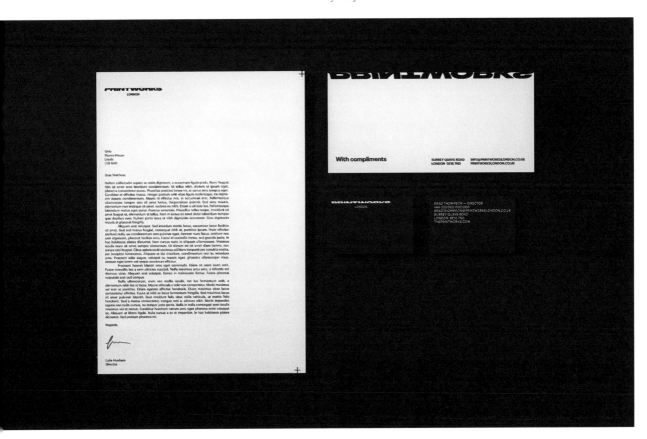

Cemento

by S-T

S-T is a London-based creative design agency that was founded in 2012. By intentionally remaining a small team, S-T's core members are able to stay as immersed and engaged as possible in every decision-making process of a project. A close, collaborative relationship with clients is central to this approach. They've worked alongside organizations including the Royal Academy of Arts, Laurence King Publishing, *The Times* and Arcadia Group on wide-ranging projects involving branding, art direction, editorial and web design, illustration, animation, packaging design and more.

Cemento is an Italian-made composite concrete product that is lightweight and comes in the form of a veneered panel. It can be applied to exterior and interior walls and ceilings but doesn't rely on the laborious process of installing heavy, wet concrete, saving time and money but achieving the same visual outcome. In 2013, the material's UK distributor asked S-T to design an identity that would appeal within their markets. The result mirrors the square format of the panelling with a simple, bold C-like symbol, which is paired with clean, modern typography to create a luxury look that also feels informal – just like the product itself.

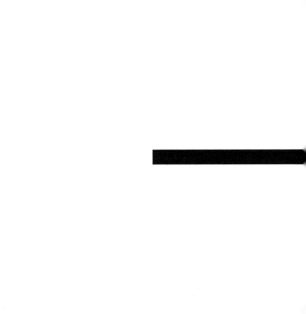

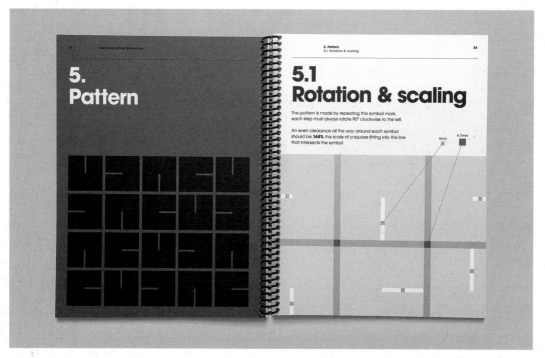

Cemento is functional and precise yet at the same time achieves
a beauty of form that has echoes of Brutalism, and S-T's design
direction succeeds in reflecting this dual personality. Like all good
identities focused around a particular product, it makes sure that
the material takes centre stage. The monochrome colour palette
is a natural fit with Cemento's concrete-like properties; anything
else might feel jarring and disruptive. A repeating, rotating pattern
cleverly evokes the gridded effect of the installed panels and adds
a playful, highly graphic edge.

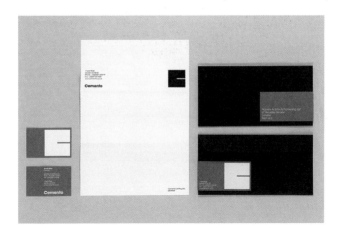

1 Sans Walk
London EC1R 0LT
Tel: +44 (0)20 2552141
www.cemento.co.uk

Cemento UK Ltd is the UK partner of the Italian company
Sai Industry which has developed the revolutionary
concrete product known as Cemento. Patent pending.

Sai Industry's creation, Cemento is a lightweight
and Eco concrete suitable for endless applications,
both interior and exterior.

- **Natural product**
  - No resins used
- **Suitable for interior or exterior**
- **Lightweight**
  - No structural reinforcement required
- **Short lead-time**
  - 4wks standard from order
- **Environmental and sustainable**
  - Certified by the international lab UL.com
- **Vast range of colours**
  - Any RAL, NCS or Pantone colours can be added
  - to the natural concrete
- **Choice of textures and finishes**
- **Dry install**
  - No mess or wet trades required
- **Panels can easily accommodate site changes**
  - Scribing, extra cut outs etc
- **Flexible curved sheets available**
  - Minimum curved radius 50mm
- **Fast install**
  - Using Q-Clip system
- **ECO Cores**
  - All timber substrates meet EU timber regulations
- **Removable and reusable**

1 Sans Walk
London EC1R 0LT
Tel: +44 (0)207 2052141
www.cemento.co.uk

Cemento

Cemento

Basement Theatre

by Studio Alexander

Founded in 1999, Studio Alexander is a design studio based in Auckland, New Zealand, that puts an emphasis on strategy. While aiming to maintain a youthful approach to any and all briefs – including brand identities for clients such as craftsman Carin Wilson and homebrew beer kit company WilliamsWarn – Studio Alexander also bring their extensive experience to bear across all their projects.

Theatres, in the traditional sense, can be a little stuck in their ways. Historically, designers working to help promote stage shows have opted for tried-and-tested, full-bleed photographic posters featuring the show's stars. Progressive design systems can be a difficult sell for consumers in this area but, fortunately, Studio Alexander's thoughtful concept for Basement Theatre, also located in Auckland, was embraced. It gives the venue a daring, modern edge and displays a clear attempt to engage a younger audience.

The clever 'stairs' icon is made from joining two letter 'T's together, and the overall art direction almost appears influenced by the fashion world. The punchy colour palette, comprising vibrant pinks, greens and blues, creates impact and consistency across various collateral materials. Trying to reconcile a range of photography from different productions can be tricky, and this solution provides a sense of unity across disparate shows and seasons.

BASEMENT THEATRE ®

Indep- endent theatre for our comm- unity.

Yes you...

basementtheatre.co.nz

join the list, get in touch.

BASEMENT THEATRE

Walter Knoll

by Systems Studio

Systems is a London-based studio with a focus on graphic design for print, web, wayfinding and environments. Working for clients in the cultural sector, the studio draws together experience and insights from various fields, including industrial design, philosophy and fine art. These diverse influences inform Systems's approach and graphic output: the designers maintain a level of creative freedom and are able to explore and execute work with an abstract, conceptual methodology.

In addition to traditional studio work, Systems also produce exhibitions and other design-related events. In 2013, long-established German furniture company Walter Knoll commissioned them to curate and design a series of three exhibitions in their London showroom: 'Play', which displayed modernist toys from British designers of the 1960s; 'Unfeasible', an exhibition of speculative architecture consisting of proposals by ten leading architectural practices; and 'Undone', a show of sculptural works. This brief created an interesting challenge, as each exhibition needed to have its own voice but also sit well alongside the others in a space that is usually used to display furniture. Systems solved this problem by playing up the fact that the shows are inextricably linked, achieving this through the use of a consistent blind deboss on all promotional materials. When seen in the context of the catalogue's cover, everything joins up perfectly.

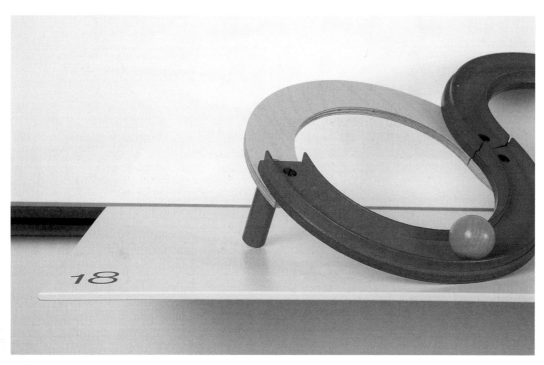

WALTER KNOLL

Vanity

Fraa Atelier have designed a new office for themselves. The project
is unrealisable because they're really quite satisfied with their present
accommodation. Despite this, the architects can't help wondering
about the office they don't have. This project has the form of pure
speculation; a romantic wishing without an object.

Intangible

Stanton Williams
of four seminal Int
Design at Lond'
and What's Profi
of interventions
In the absence o
has itself becom
the final outline

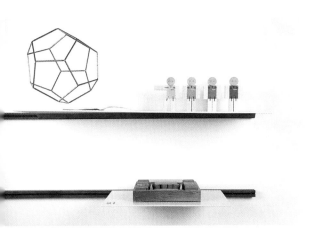

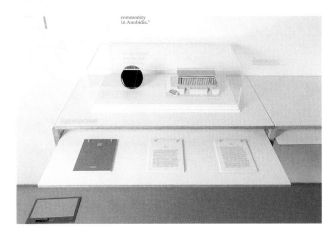

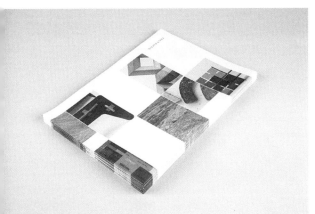

Inside, the loose-leaf catalogue focuses on abstract crops and teaser imagery of content associated with the exhibitions, which is well considered, since giving too much away before a show can run the risk of deterring visitors. The worlds of art, furniture design, product design, architecture and craft have been pulled together through a unified visual language. The power of graphic design to properly represent all these sectors at once shows how important it is to design from a holistic perspective.

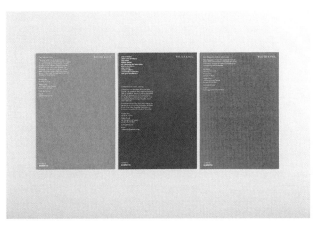

G.F Smith

by Studio Makgill

Often seen as the premier paper supplier for the creative industries, G.F Smith have been making and selling truly unique paper stocks of exceptional quality since 1885. They have established an engaged vision that has seen them get involved with cultural projects and other companies at a grassroots level, supporting them by providing free paper and promotion in exchange for brand awareness and loyalty. Those artists and designers supported by the firm then look to G.F Smith when paid jobs eventually come through the door.

Working alongside design consultancy Made Thought, in 2014 Studio Makgill (see page 78) were commissioned to create a new visual identity to span all areas of G.F Smith's vast business. The opportunity to create a design system around such a considerable range of materials opens up endless possibilities – but, as a primarily industry-facing project, it could also feel like a daunting task. However, the solution and revitalized identity Studio Makgill devised has streamlined the G.F. Smith brand across its entire product range into one that is succinct, clear and approachable, while representing the company's values throughout.

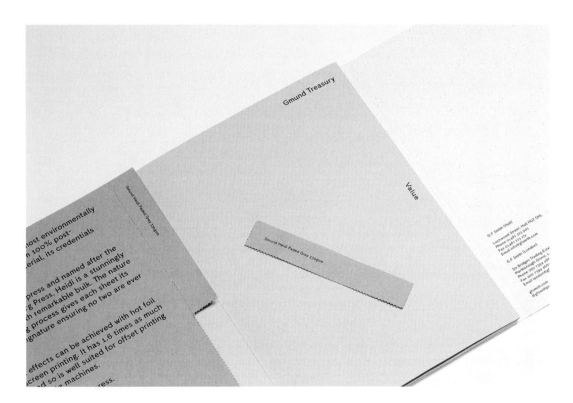

Interview with John Haslam,
managing director at G.F Smith

Do you think your own understanding of graphic design can affect
the design process, as a client?

I believe if a client feels they understand graphic design, then they
should do it themselves! We have to work with designers who
understand our requirements and challenge them. Once we are all
on the same page, they can implement creative solutions.

Colorplan
Turquoise Envelope
175gsm
from G F Smith
with metallic foil

Textures

G . F
SMITH

1885

Colorplan
Fuchsia Pink
Coltskin Embossing
270gsm
from G.F Smith

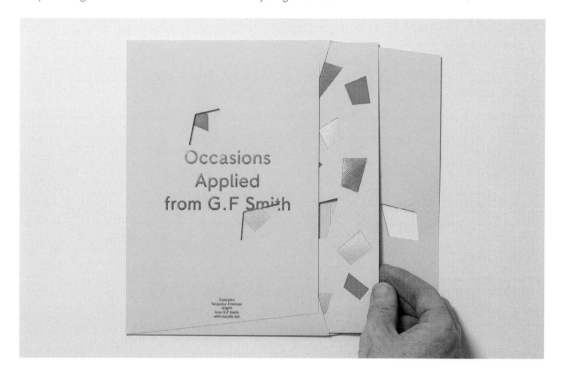

Do you find working with designers, who also operate within
the creative industries, to be easier or harder than working with
non-creatives?

> Designers design, typographers create fonts, digital agencies
> provide digital solutions, illustrators illustrate … if all these skill
> sets have compatible individual personalities, then creative output
> as a collective can be powerful. Alas, this is rare!

As a client in the creative industries, are you drawn to respond to
current trends in your field?

> It's all about the relationship. In the ideal situation, a brief is
> not always necessary and the creative partnership simply
> blossoms. Once an idea is defined it often starts a new journey.

'It's all about the relationship.
In the ideal situation, a brief is not
always necessary and the creative
partnership simply blossoms.'

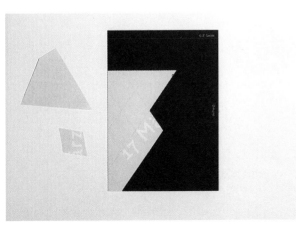

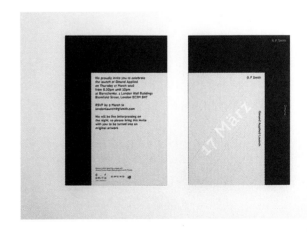

Generation Press

by Build

Creating any piece of communication for a printer as cool as
Generation Press, based in Poynings, near Brighton, UK, would be a
dream for most designers. The bountiful array of techniques to be
exploited against a plethora of paper stock choices and finishing
capabilities leaves one salivating. With their work on a suite of
direct mail items for the company, Build (see page 90) have struck a
considered, balanced tone, avoiding the temptation to go overboard,
producing a brand refresh that communicates effectively to
members of the creative industries as well as to those outside them.

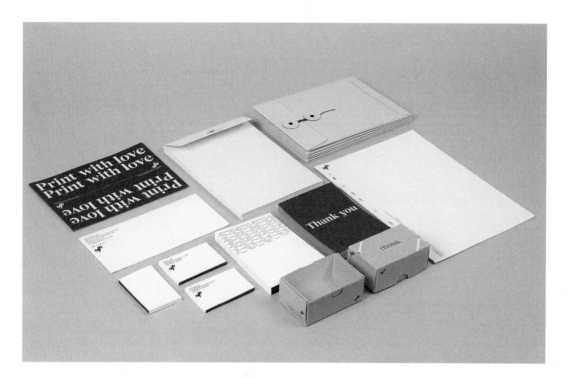

The heavy serif typeface Poynings Stencil was created specially
for this project with the help of Colophon Foundry. It is combined
with the sans serif typeface Graphik, designed by Commercial Type,
which is used for all smaller type, resulting in a helpful display
of what's possible in terms of printing scales and techniques. A
stripped-back colour palette, with grey sitting alongside a bold blue
with occasional bright red elements, gives off a sense of confidence
and works harmoniously when placed next to image-based
materials such as photographs. Accompanying copy text is witty
and engaging, helping Generation Press's available print options
makes sense to anybody.

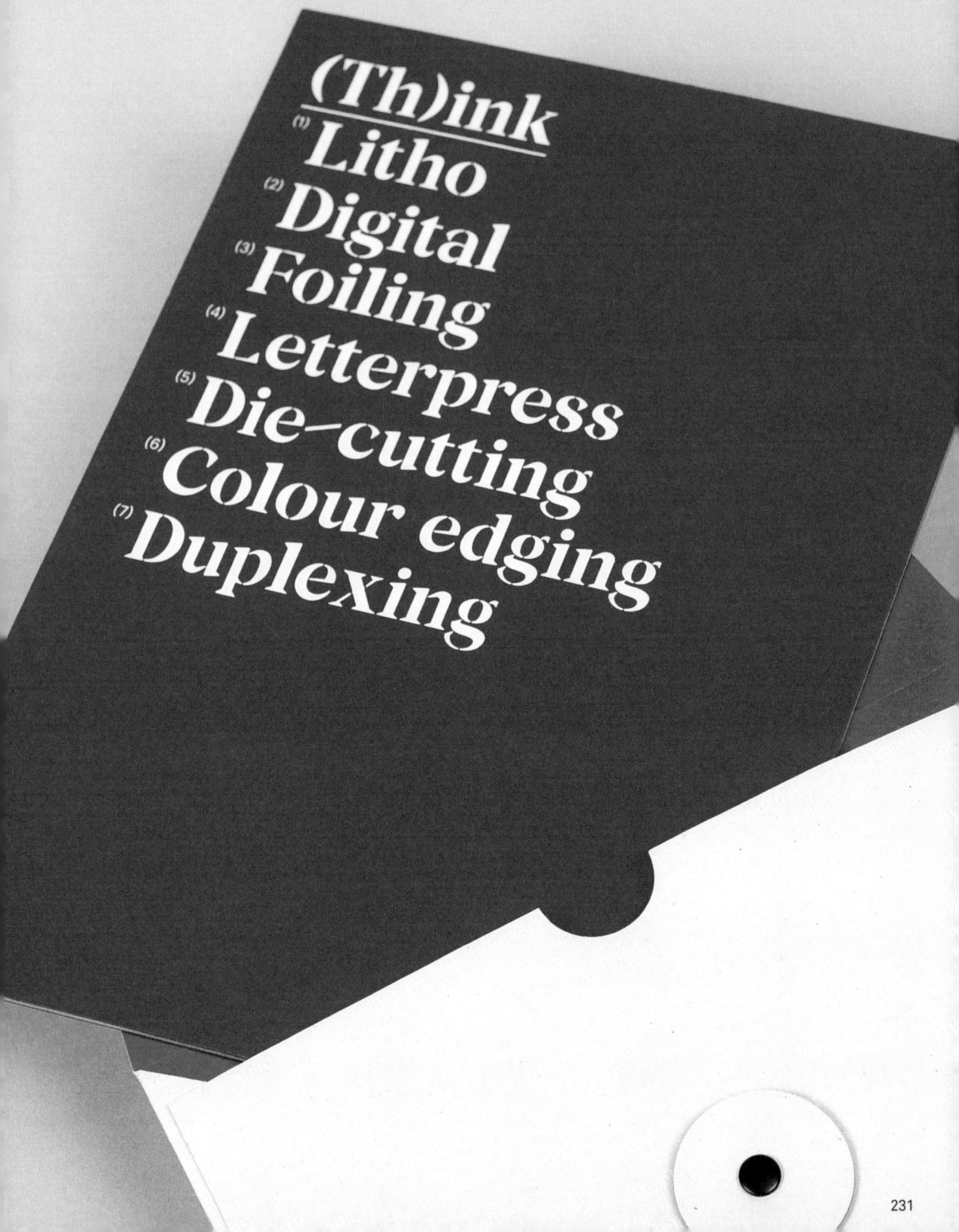

(Th)ink
(1) Litho
(2) Digital
(3) Foiling
(4) Letterpress
(5) Die–cutting
(6) Colour edging
(7) Duplexing

Interview with Michael C. Place,
creative director at Build

Do you think that crossing multiple design disciplines is a viable
approach to working within the industry today?

> Absolutely. Most creatives have really great 3D visualization skills;
> we can picture how things will sit within an environment. It's part of
> our job: the work a graphic designer produces generally sits within
> the landscape of life; it doesn't exist in isolation. It interacts with
> the world and the people who inhabit it. Graphic design isn't always
> passive; it's not something that exists in a 2D form. So, could a
> graphic designer create a piece of furniture? You bet!

Does your design process differ when you're dealing with a client
within the creative industries?

> It does a little, in a couple of ways. A creative client looks at the
> work in a very different way than a non-creative client. They seem
> to want to connect with the work in a much more philosophical
> and personal way. These clients are commercial entities, but
> the connection generally doesn't seem to focus on the return on
> investment. Creative clients historically, for us, also seem to worry
> a lot more about how their peers will respond to a piece of work.
> Clients outside the sector fall into two camps: ones who have a gut
> feeling about a piece of design, and those that analyse it to death in
> a very clinical way. Design as joy versus design as commodity.

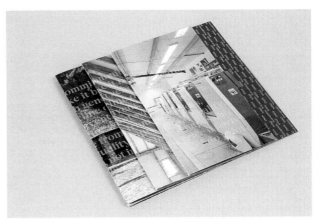

How much does a client's understanding of graphic design affect the design process?

It can affect it massively. For the most part it is a bonus, but it can also be a hindrance. We always say: enter into the process with an open mind. Come to the party not with a completed jigsaw, but with one unboxed (and if there is a piece missing, that's cool too). The journey is the fun bit. If you already know the destination, where is the fun in that? Getting lost is fun; being found when you are lost is an amazing feeling.

The journey is the fun bit. If you already know the destination, where is the fun in that? Getting lost is fun; being found when you are lost is an amazing feeling.'

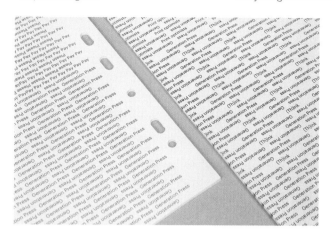

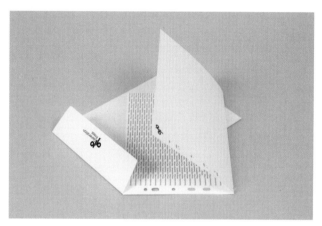

Every potential client now has access to software that can output graphic design, in some form, at their fingertips. How has this impacted the way we design for design-savvy clients?

> I don't personally believe that it makes one bit of difference. People have always had the tools to output graphic design (pens and pencils, for example); it's our job to steer them in a direction in which they might not have thought to go. The path less travelled is often the most rewarding.

How do we communicate graphic design's core value to creative clients when this is the case?

> Take their pens, pencils and computers away from them? In the end, though, those are just tools. Graphic design is a way of looking at the world, how we perceive the world. No amount of fancy tools will beat that; good graphic design is not a dot-to-dot world. It's about passion and determination and the willingness to listen – and to ignore, if that's what it takes.

Do you feel designers must expand their technology-based skill
sets to stay relevant?

Possibly. But clients will always need people with an idea.

How do you see graphic design's role in the wider creative
industries, traditionally and in the future?

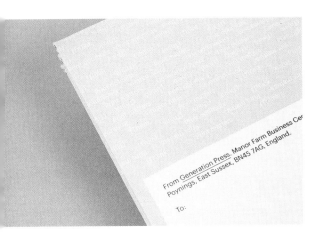

The obvious answer would be to see it move further off paper
and onto the screen. The industry is much more connected now;
different disciplines work together and not in isolation. The role of
the graphic designer has always been a valuable one. As time has
passed, that role has been more widely recognized by the general
public – and not always in a positive light. Graphic design is cruelly
undervalued given the importance it plays in our daily lives. With the
meteoric rise of the personal computer it may seem like everyone
is a designer and that they could do it better than a so-called
professional.

Traditionally, the role of the graphic designer is like
that of a shepherd, who quietly and gently (with the help of a
sheepdog) points the sheep in the right direction. We used to do
this by designing print advertising, wayfinding systems, corporate
identities and so on. The future will largely be screen-based, placing
massive importance on user experience and user interface design.
The same shit really, different medium. In the future, printed pieces
will become a coveted luxury, because people can become much
more emotionally attached to them. Things with longevity built into
them equals more emotional attachment.

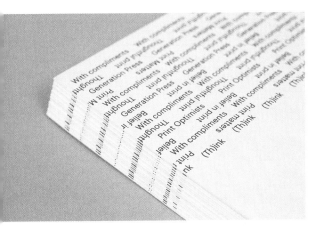

'Graphic design is a way of looking at
the world, how we perceive the world.'

Art

ArtRabbit by Bond
client: artrabbit.com / studio: bond-agency.com

Edouard Malingue Gallery by Lundgren+Lindqvist
client: edouardmalingue.com / studio: lundgrenlindqvist.se

Haus der Kunst by Base
client: hausderkunst.de / studio: basedesign.com

ArtDate by Studio Temp
client: theblank.it / studio: madeintemp.com

Art Museum at the University of Toronto by Underline Studio
client: artmuseum.utoronto.ca / studio: underlinestudio.com

Fashion

Augustus Pili by Koto
client: augustus-pili.myshopify.com / studio: studiokoto.co

Smets by Coast
client: smets.lu / studio: coast-agency.com

Bespoke by DIA
client: bespokedigital.com / studio: dia.tv

Arrels by Hey
client: arrelsbarcelona.com / studio: heystudio.es

Nike by Hort
client: nike.com / studio: hort.org.uk

STÓR by SocioDesign
client: stor.supply / studio: sociodesign.co.uk

Boxpark by Studio Makgill
client: Boxpark.co.uk / studio: studiomakgill.com

Film

Momento Film by Bedow
client: momentofilm.se / studio: bedow.se

3angrymen by Build
client: 3angrymen.com / studio: studio.build

Reel by Richards Partners
client: reel.productions (now brewery.studio) / studio: richards.partners

Storyline Studios by Work in Progress
client: storyline.no / studio: workinprogress.no

Architecture

This Brutal House by Peter Chadwick
client: thisbrutalhouse.com / studio: popularuk.com

Fraher Architects by Freytag Anderson
client: fraher.co / studio: freytaganderson.com

Rainer Schmidt Landscape Architects by Hort
client: rainerschmidt.com / studio: hort.org.uk

Laand by Passport
client: laand.co.uk / studio: wearepassport.com

North Glasgow College by Endpoint
client: glasgowkelvin.ac.uk / studio: weareendpoint.com

Hunger by The Full Service
client: hungertv.com / studio: thefullservice.co.uk

Ali Sharaf by Mash Creative
client: alisharaf.com / studio: mashcreative.co.uk

David Rowland by ico Design
client: davidrowland.photo / studio: icodesign.com

Room Essentials by Collins
client: target.com/bp/room+essentials / studio: wearecollins.com

DOIY by Folch
client: doiydesign.com / studio: folchstudio.com

ByALEX by Alex Swain
client: byalex.co.uk / studio: byalex.co.uk

Finchtail by Believe in®
client: finchtail.com / studio: believein.net

Bec Brittain by Lotta Nieminen
client: becbrittain.com / studio: lottanieminen.com

Printworks by Only
client: printworkslondon.co.uk / studio: onlystudio.co.uk

Cemento by S-T
client: cemento.co.uk / studio: designbyst.com

Basement Theatre by Studio Alexander
client: basementtheatre.co.nz / studio: studioalexander.co.nz

Walter Knoll by Systems Studio
client: walterknoll.de / studio: systems-studio.com

G.F Smith by Studio Makgill
client: gfsmith.com / studio: studiomakgill.com

Generation Press by Build
client: generationpress.co.uk / studio: studio.build

First and foremost, a massive thank you goes out to Ali Gitlow from Prestel for making this publication happen in the first place, and for her continued patience and understanding throughout the process. A special word of thanks to Jim Williams, my former university typography tutor, for guidance through this, as well as previous publication projects – you made me realize that it was indeed possible and that I was capable of pulling a project like this together. Thank you to the designers, clients and studios who put up with my persistent emailing and took the time to contribute their work and words of wisdom. Rob Fenton, Tom Edwards, Georgie Stanway and Paul Wainwright: as partners across various businesses and projects, thanks for bearing with me as I take on ever more jobs and tasks; I couldn't do any of it without you. Thank you to Tilly Goodier-Page at Weather for her assistance with the layouts in the design stages, as well as to my friends and family for their constant support and encouragement. And most of all, thanks to Whitney Hughes.

© Prestel Verlag, Munich · London · New York, 2018
A member of Verlagsgruppe Random House GmbH
Neumarkter Strasse 28 · 81673 Munich

Prestel Publishing Ltd.
14–17 Wells Street
London W1T 3PD

Prestel Publishing
900 Broadway, Suite 603
New York, NY 10003

Library of Congress Control Number: 2017952150
A CIP catalogue record for this book is available from the British Library.

Editorial direction: Ali Gitlow
Copyediting and proofreading: Aimee Selby
Design and layout: Andy Cooke
Production management: Friederike Schirge
Separations: Ludwig Media, Zell am See
Printing and binding: DZS
Paper: Tauro Offset

FSC
www.fsc.org

MIX
Paper from
responsible sources
FSC® C112556

Verlagsgruppe Random House FSC® N001967

Printed in Slovenia

ISBN 978-3-7913-8350-7

www.prestel.com